AF606683

Night Sketches

This book contains reproductions
of sketches taken from a notebook
made between 2004 and 2009.

Gerhard Richter
Night Sketches

HENI PUBLISHING, LONDON 2011

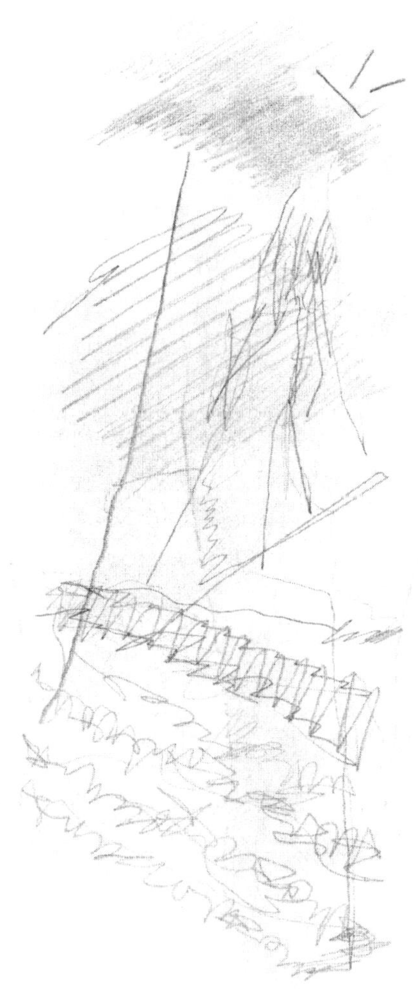

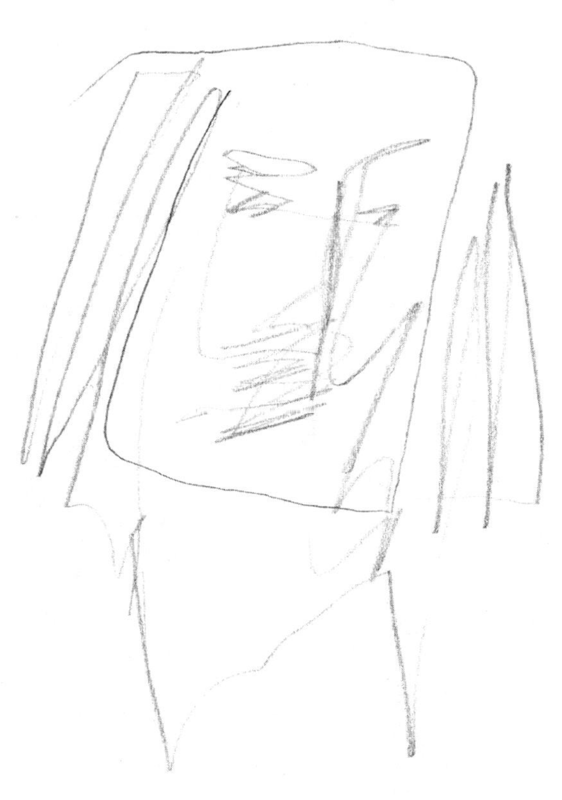

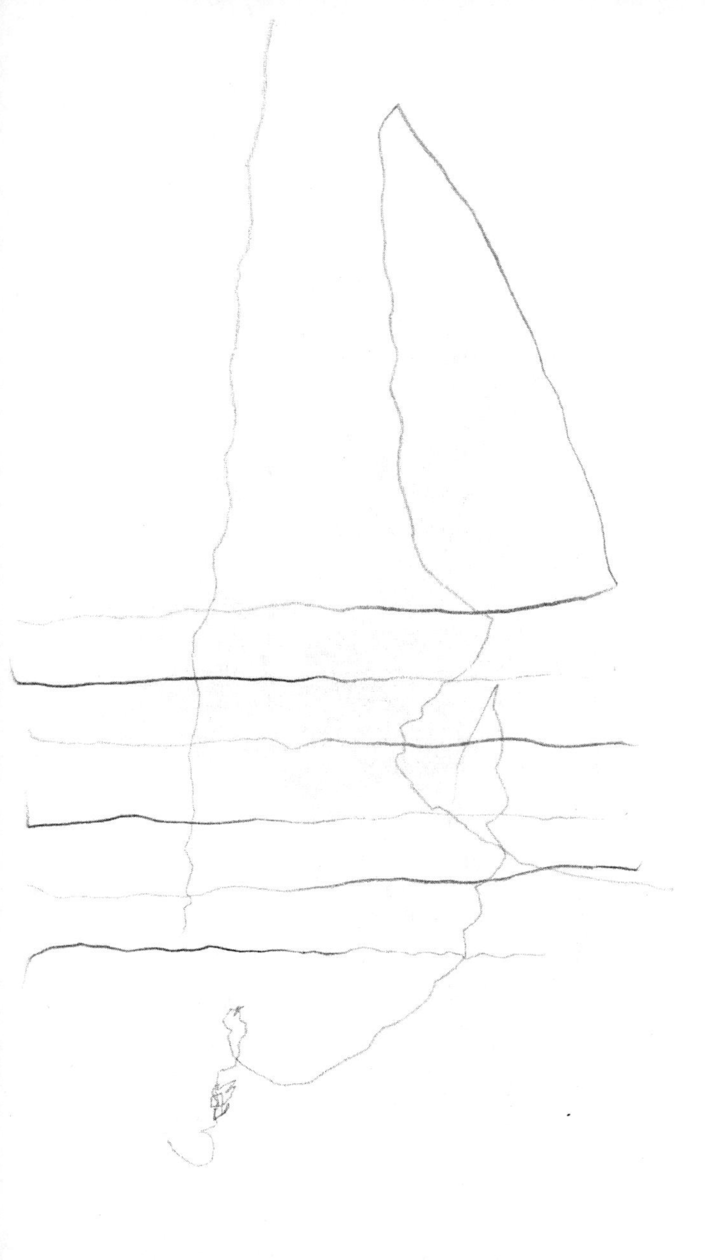

14.8.05

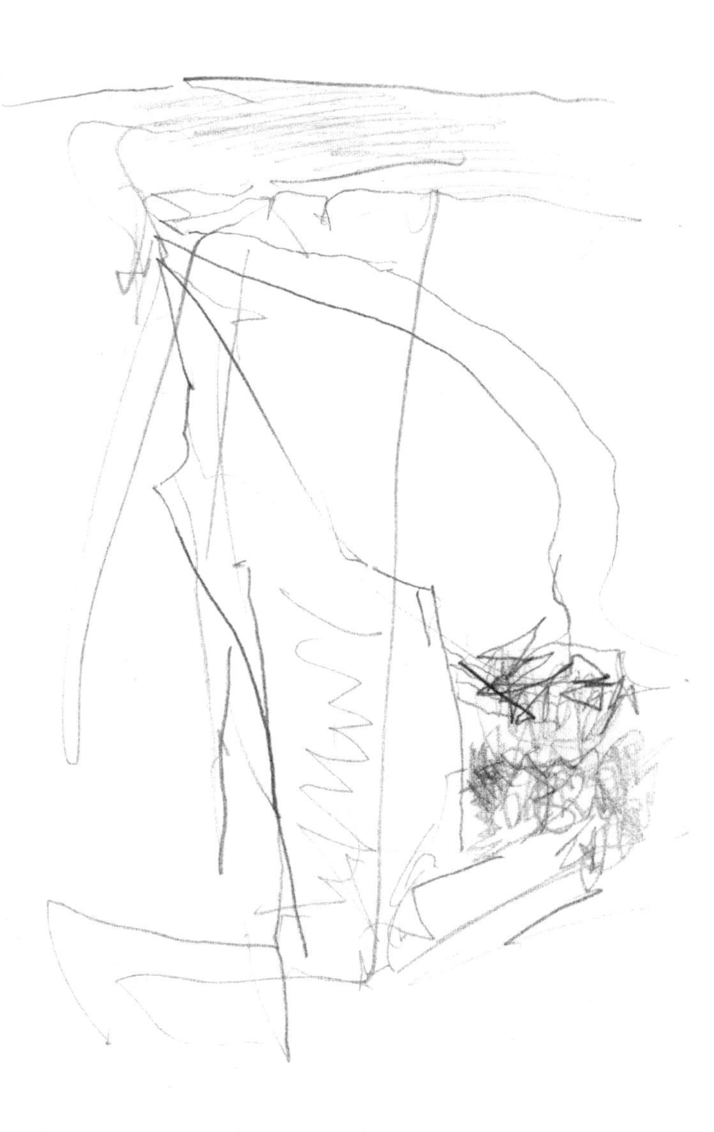

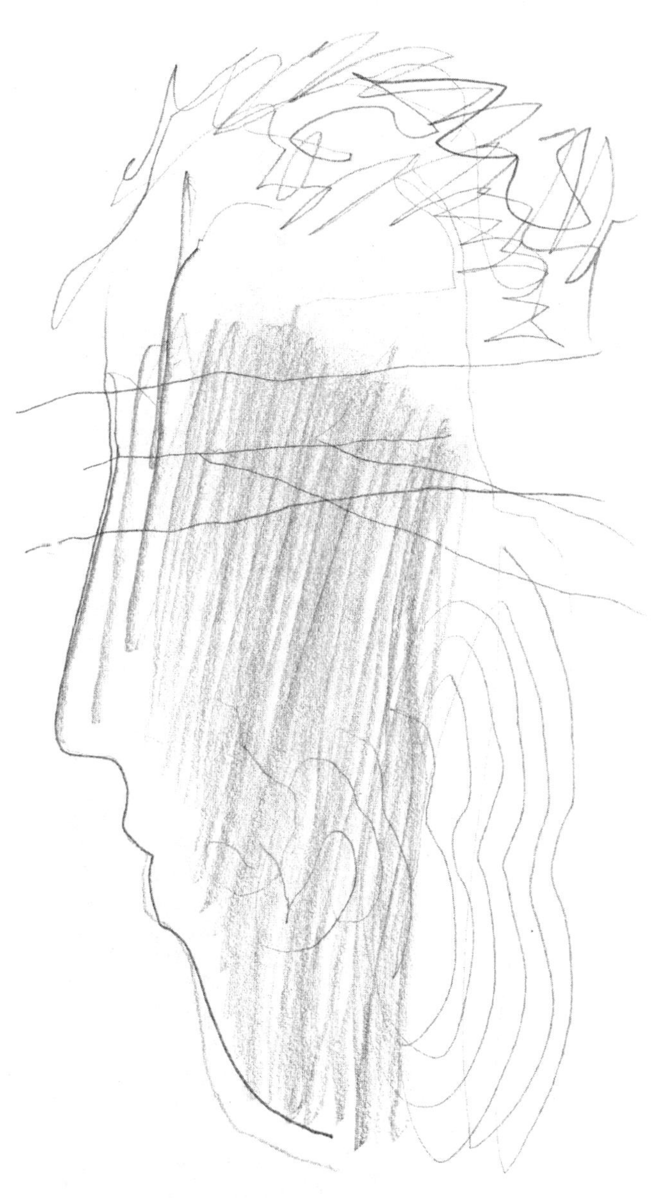

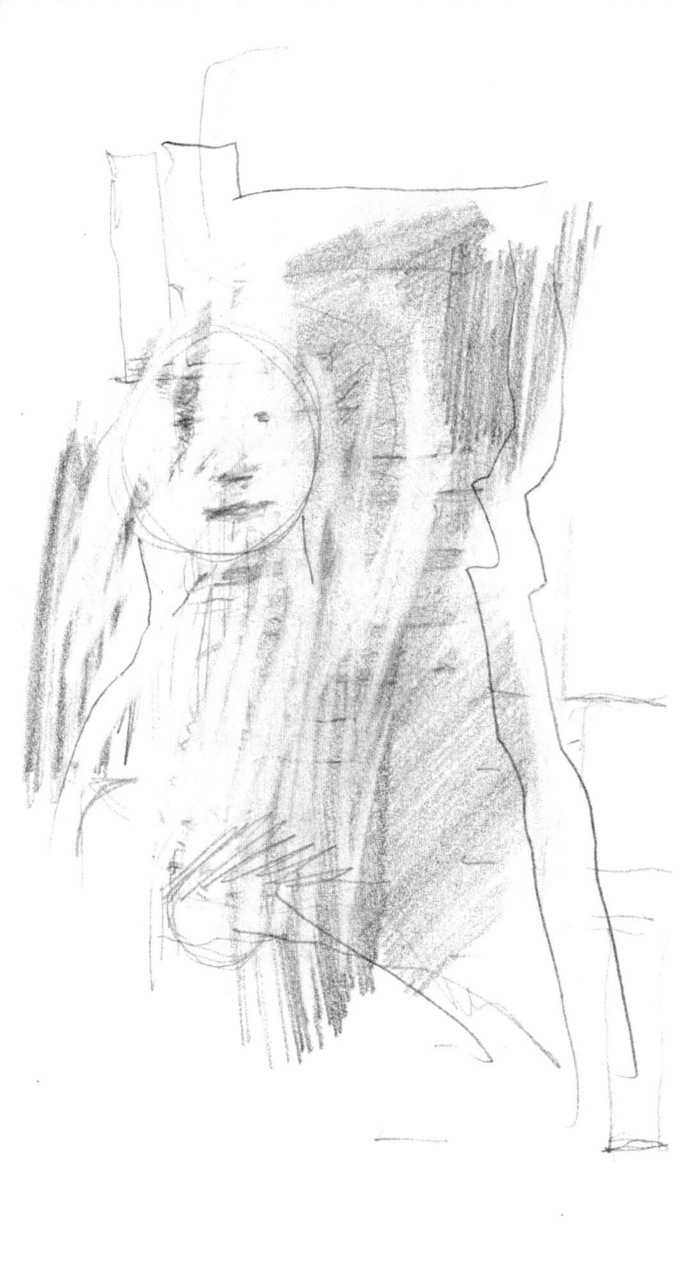

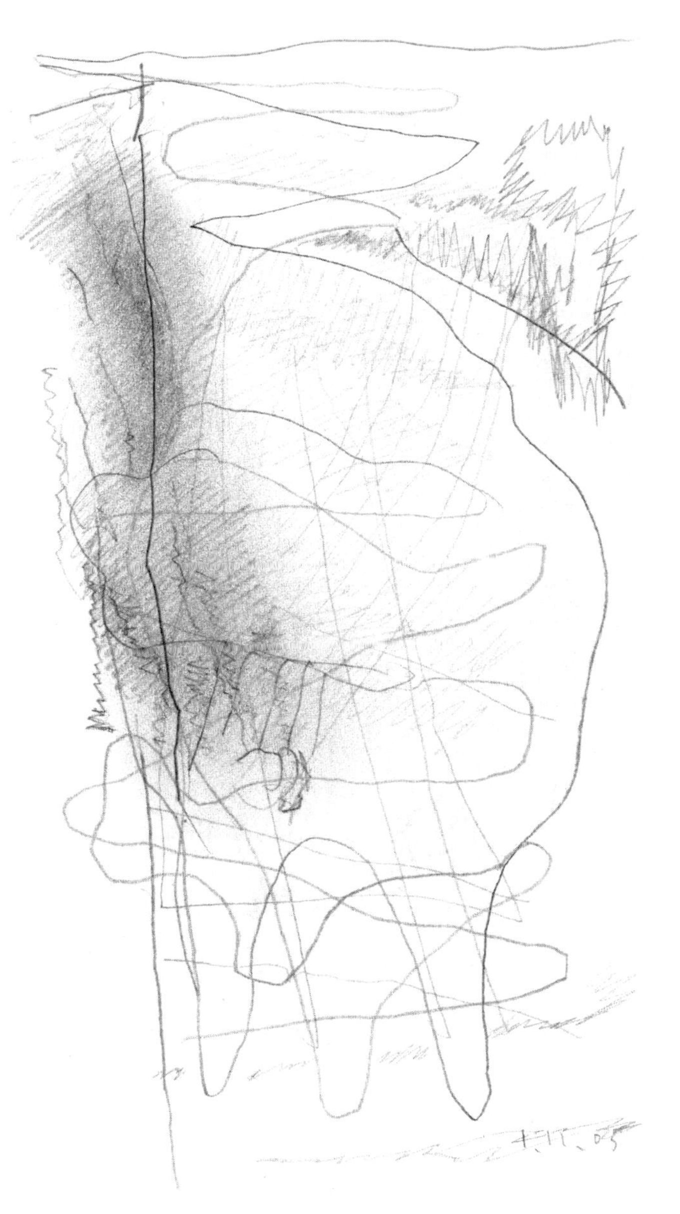

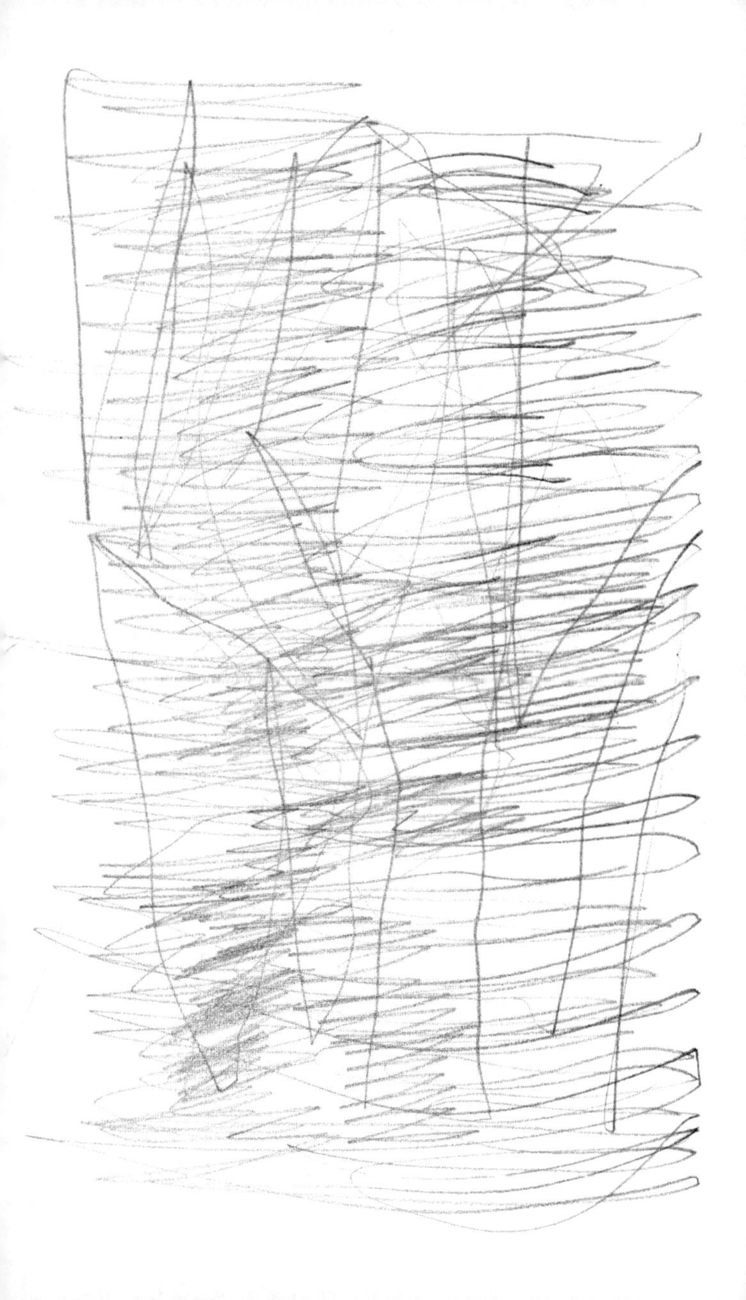

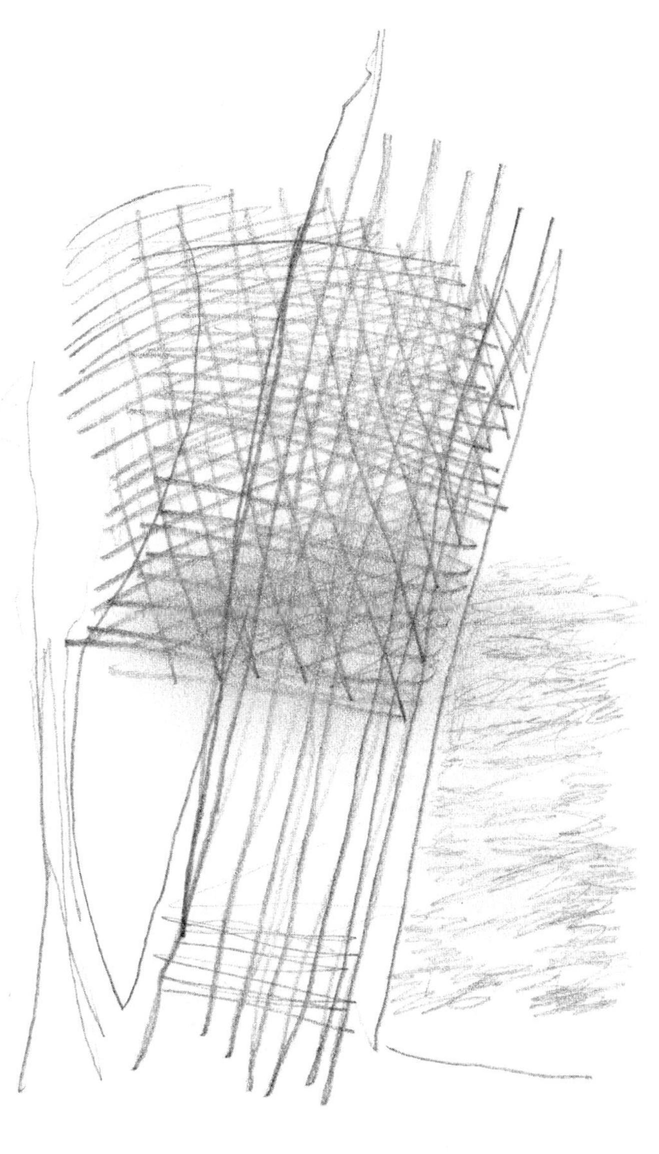

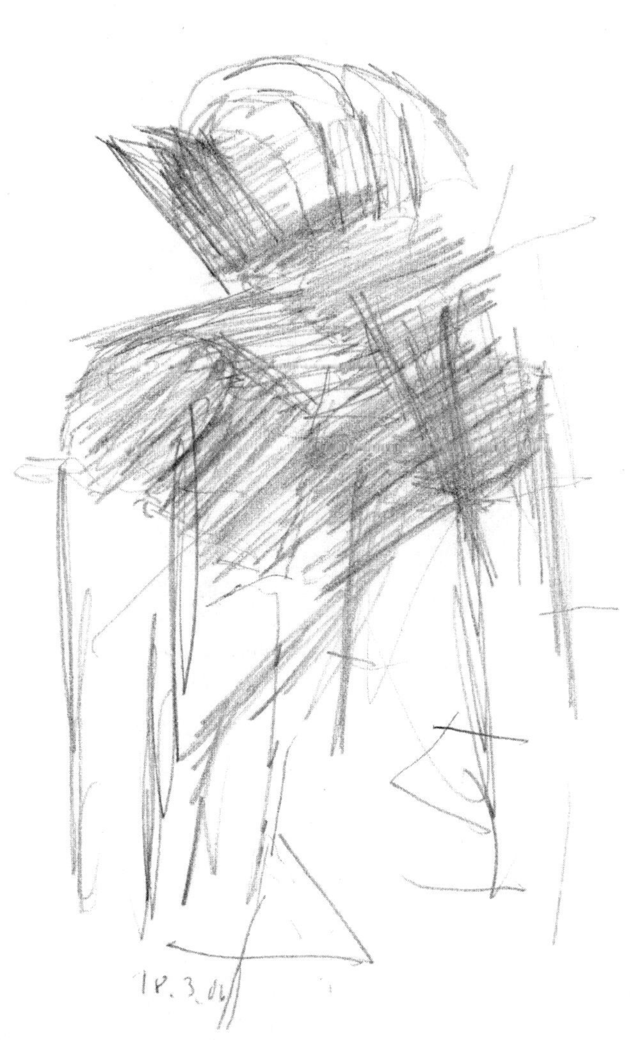
18.3.06

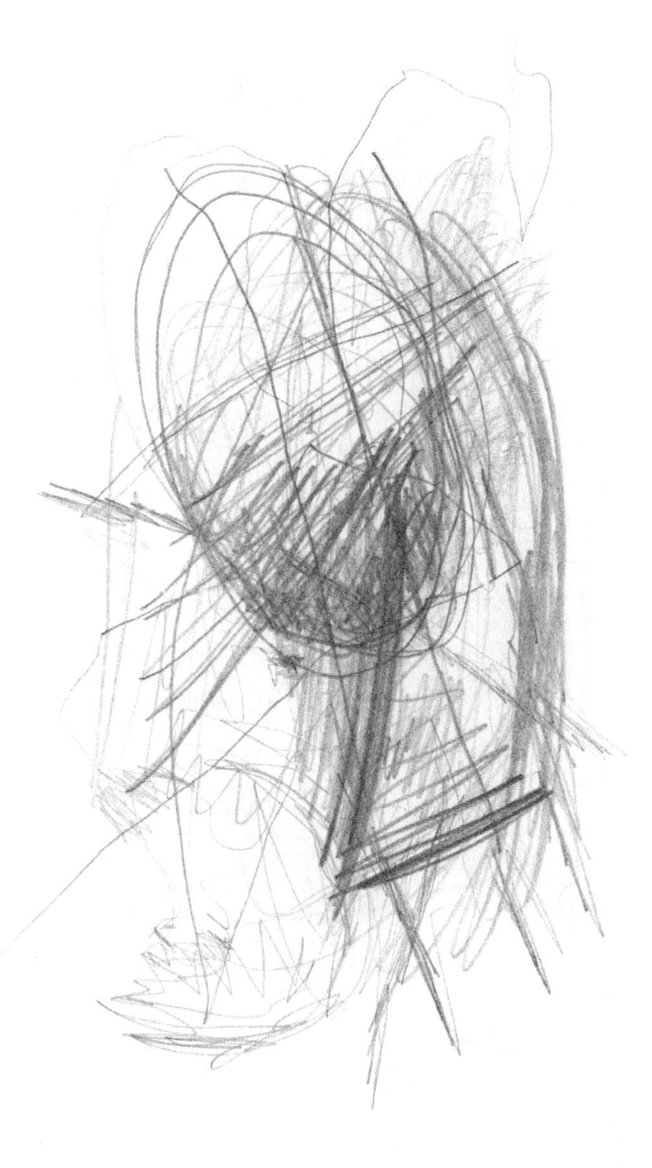

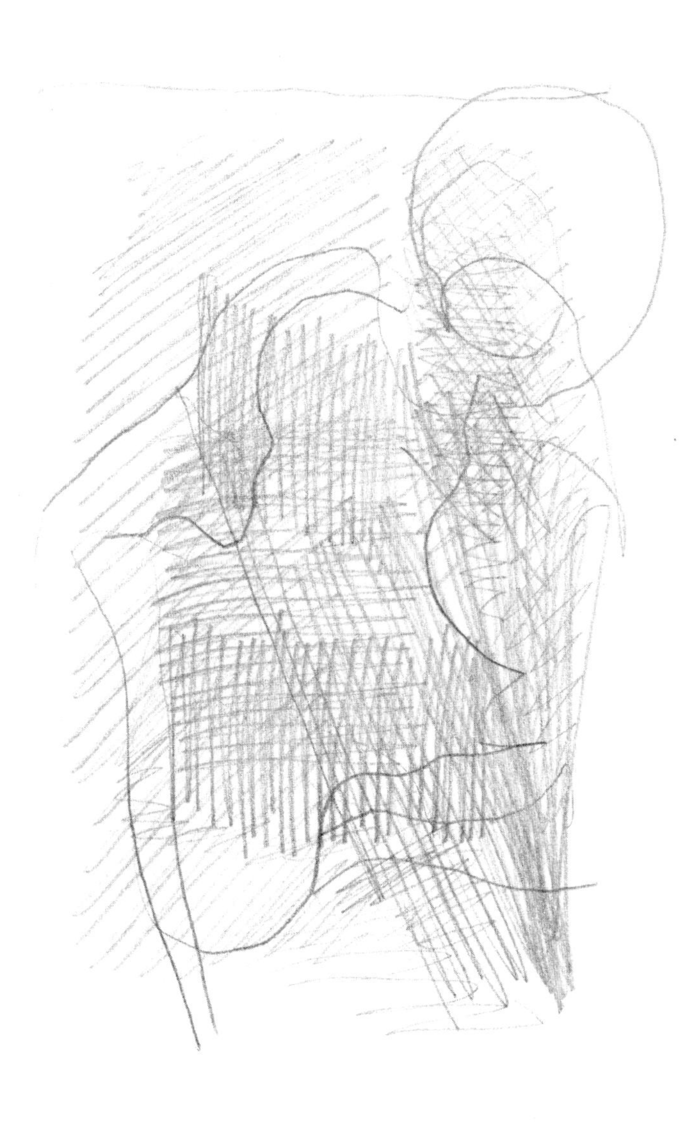

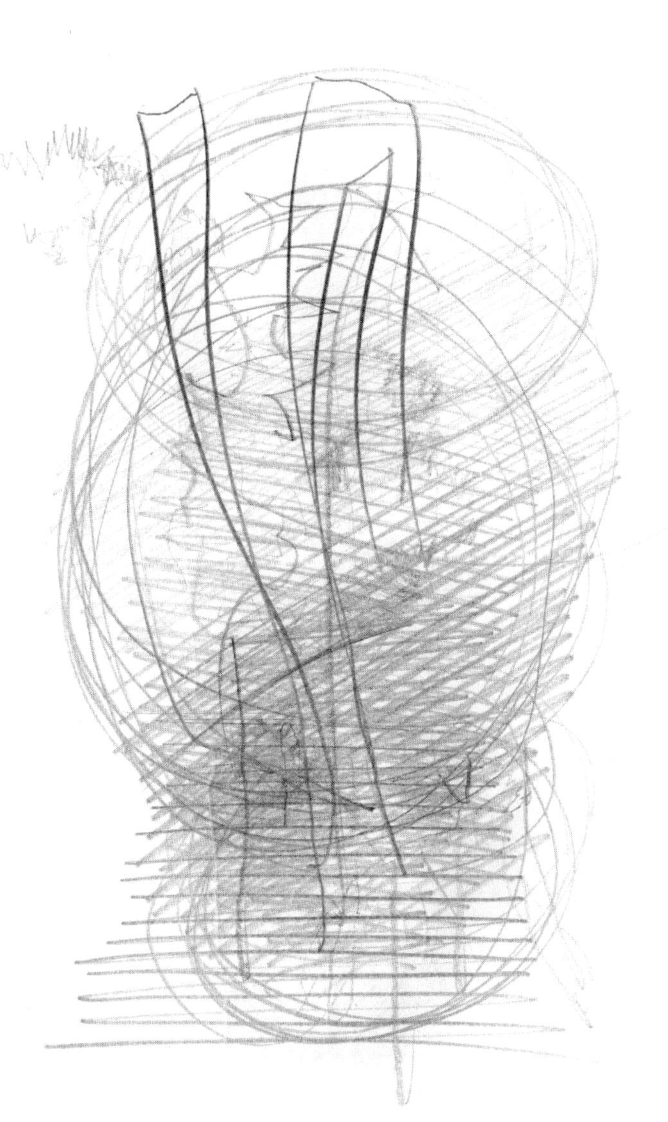

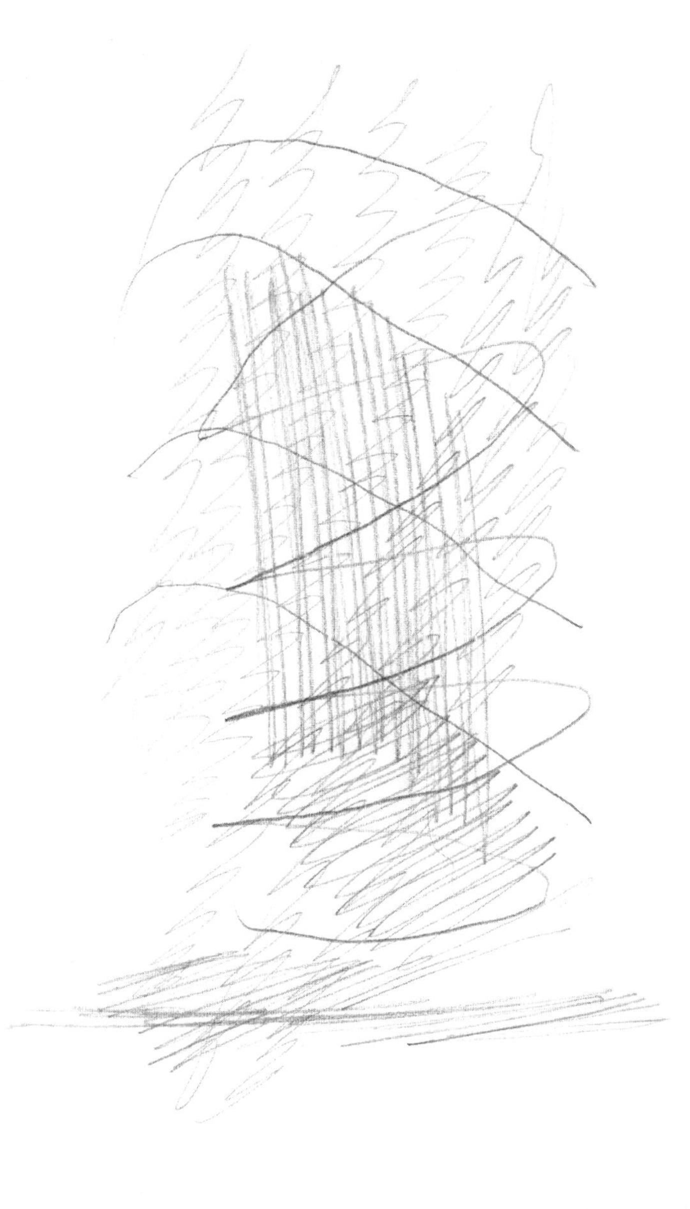

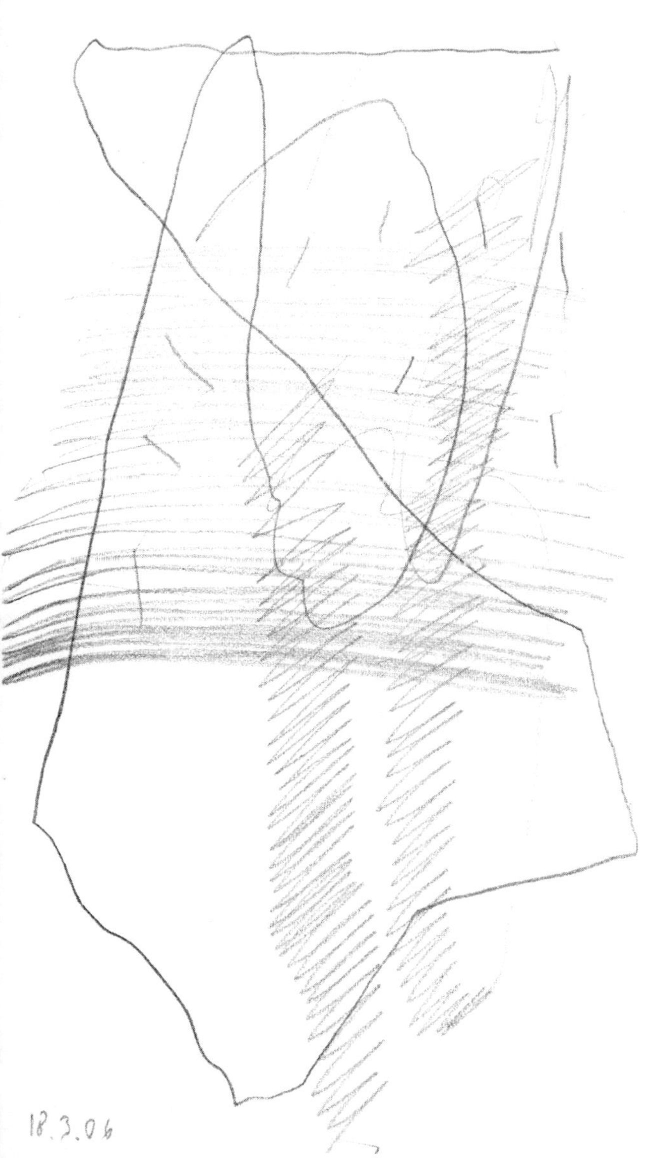
18.3.06

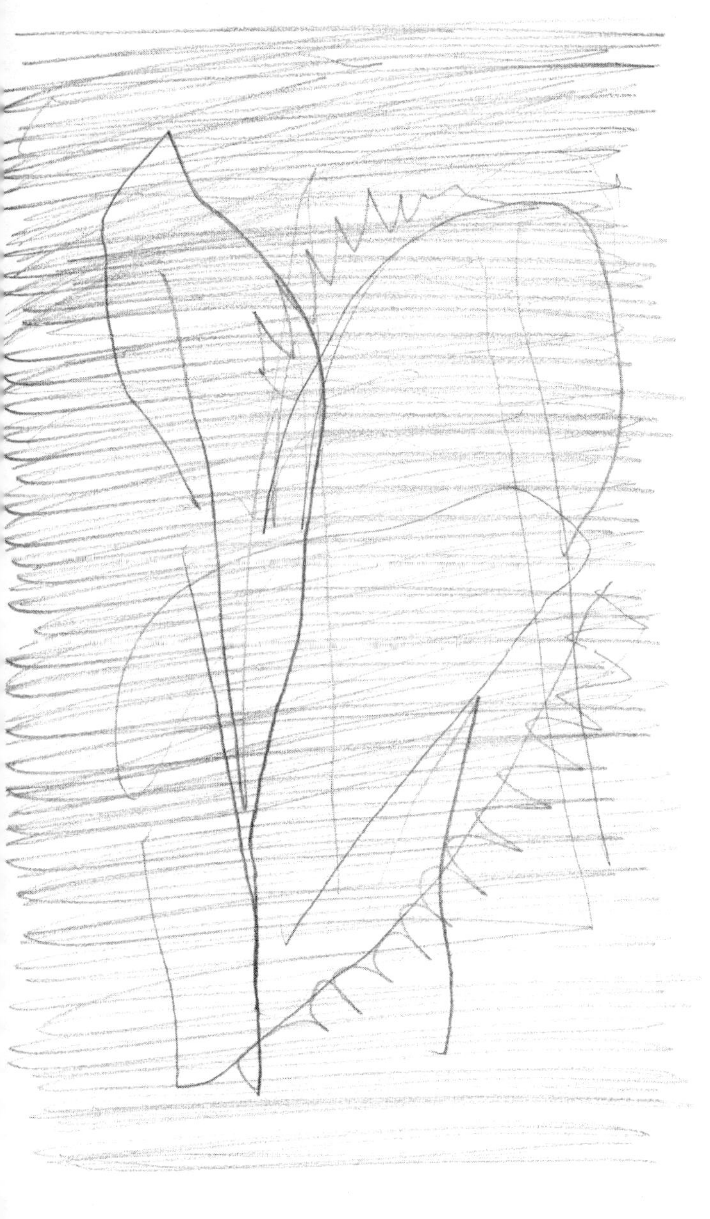

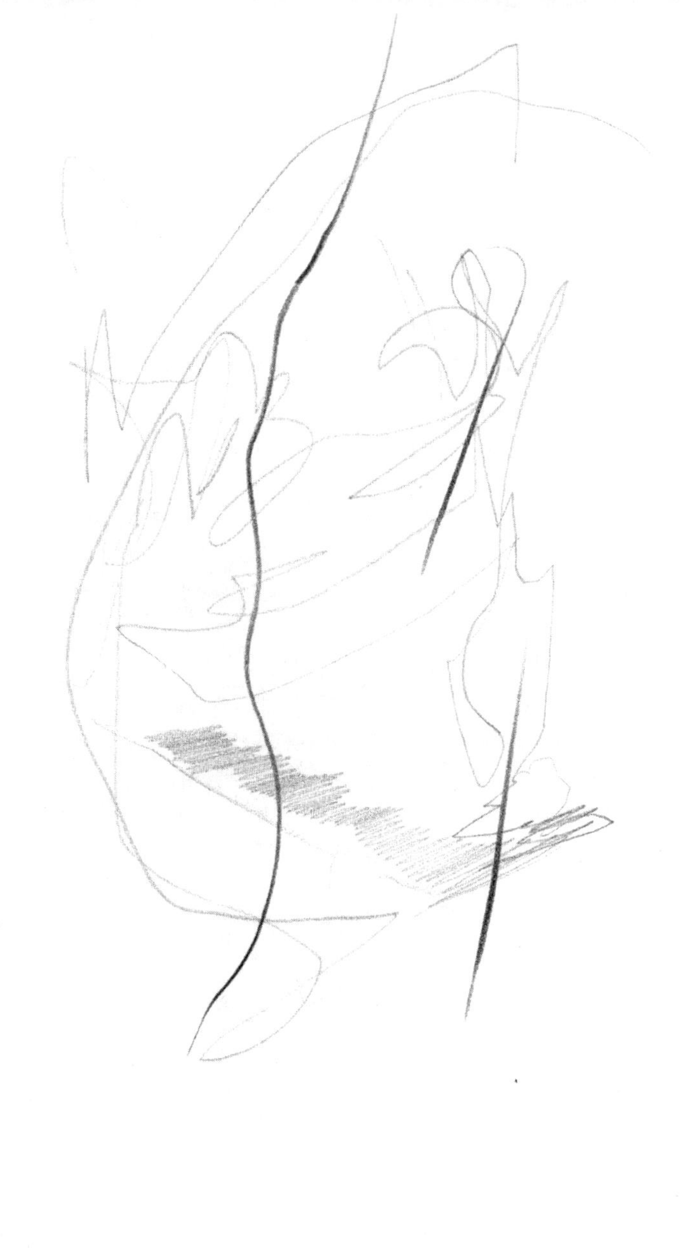

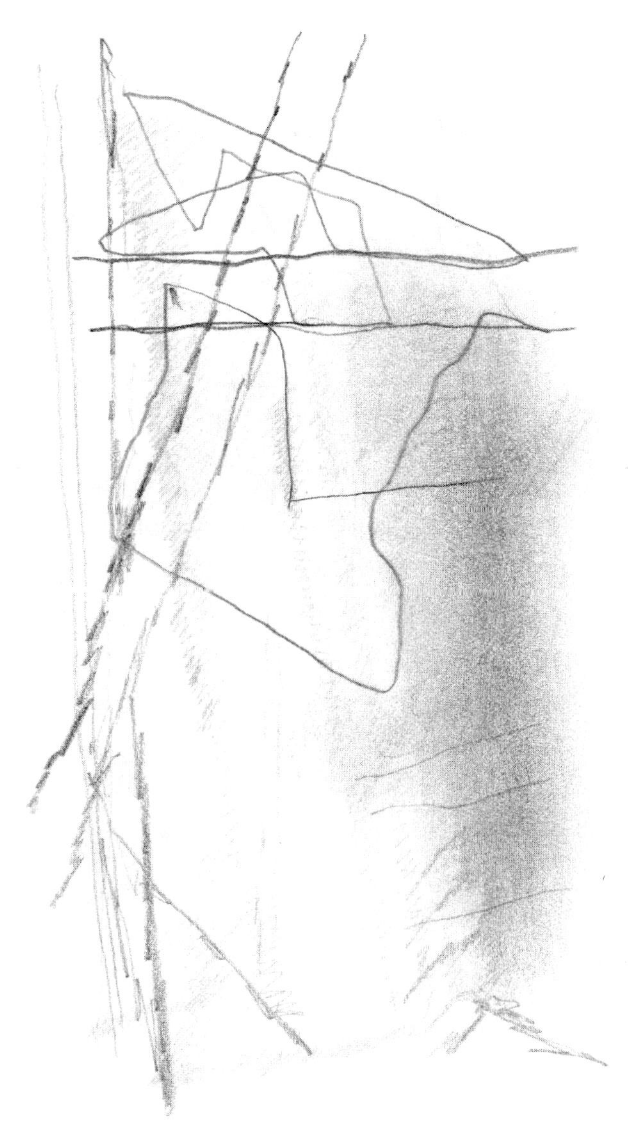

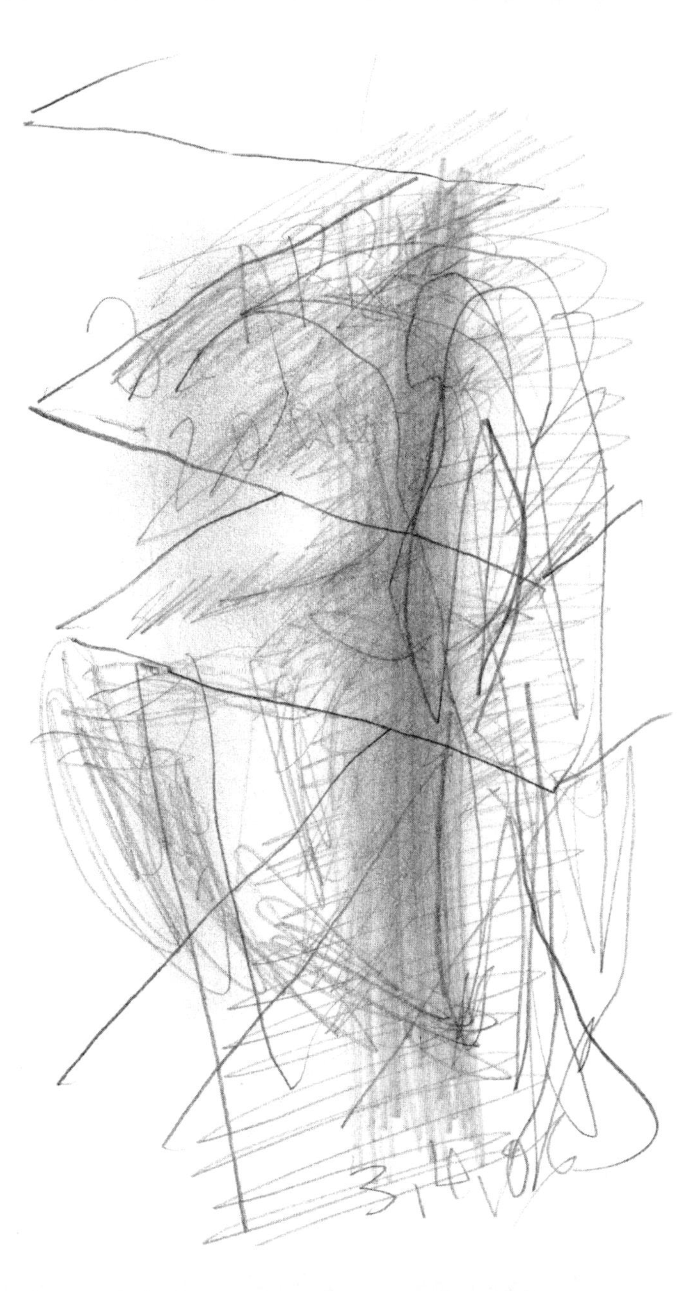

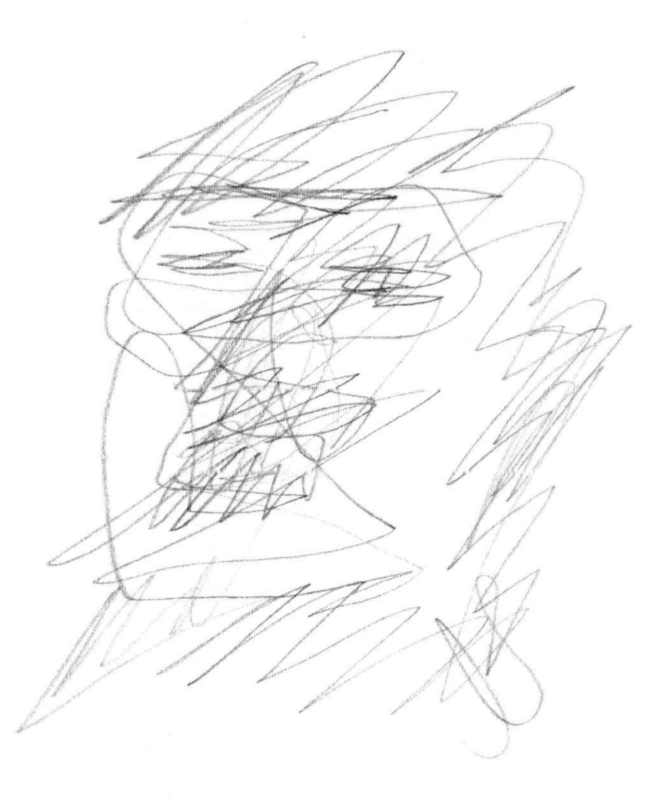

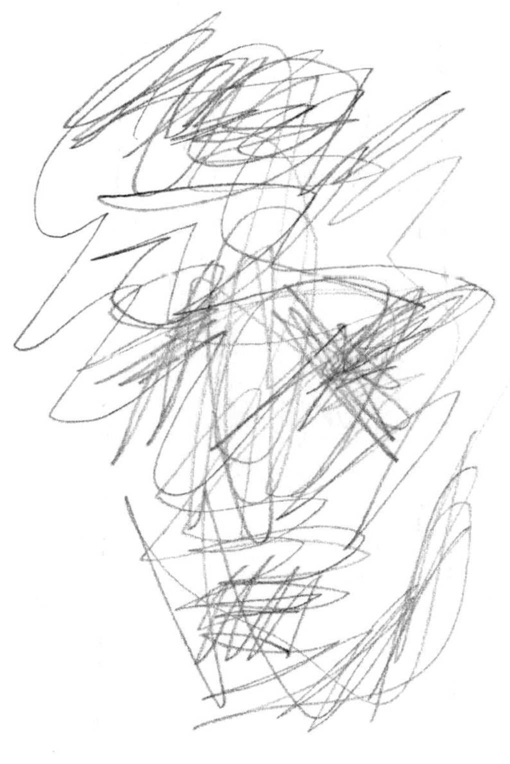

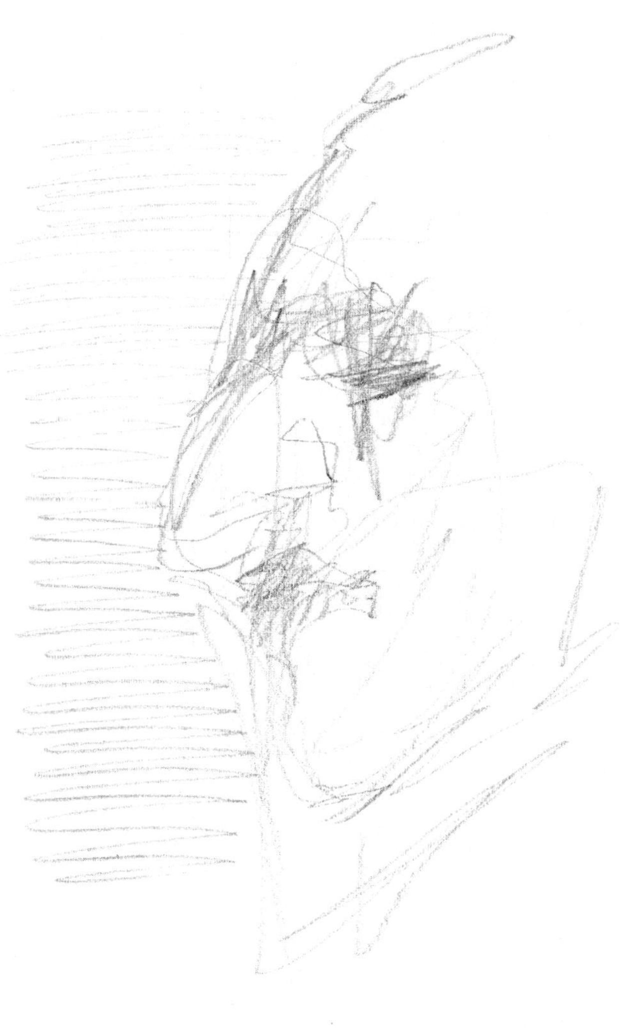

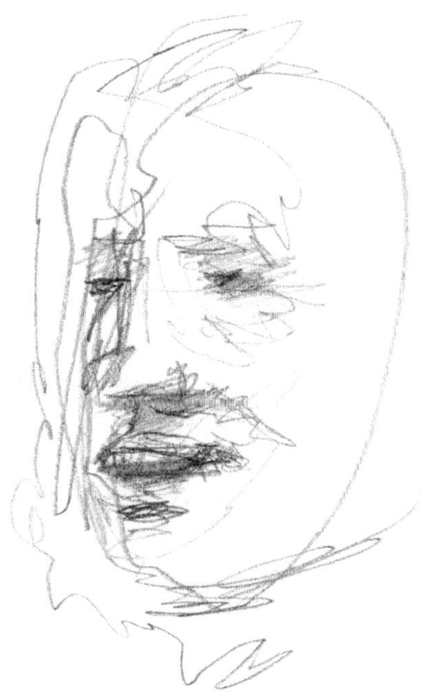

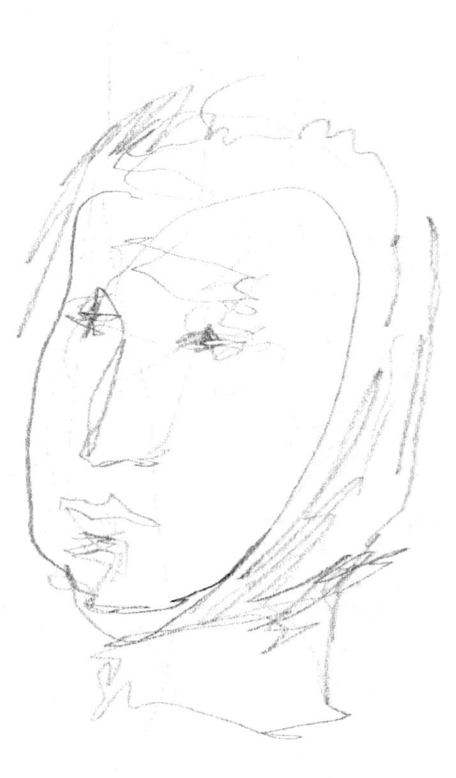

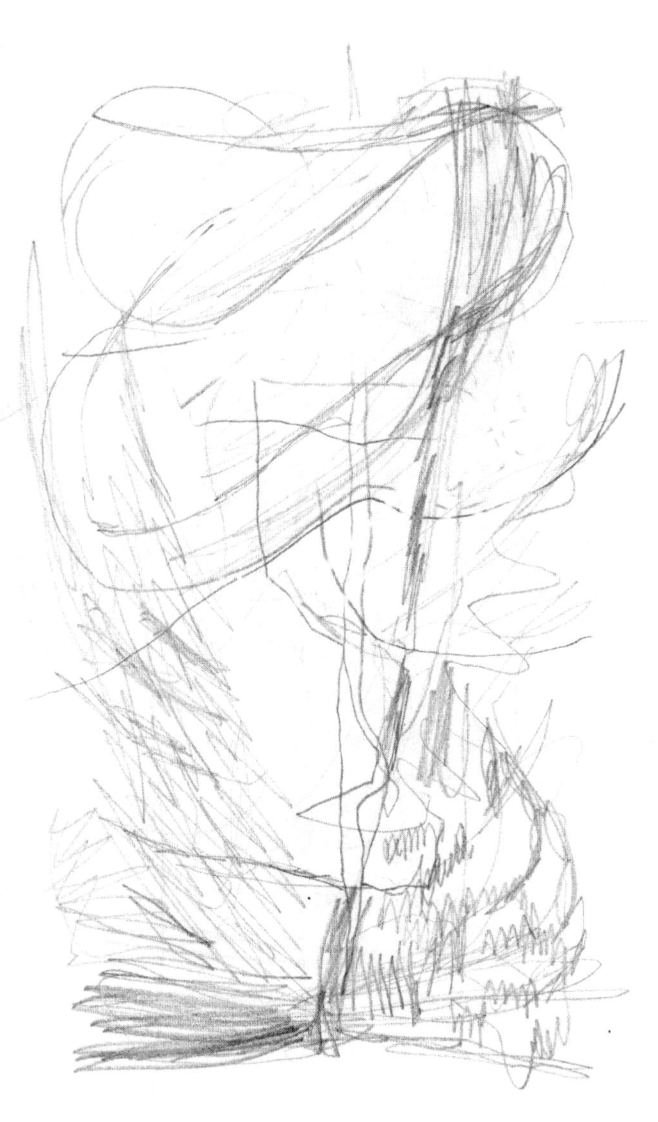

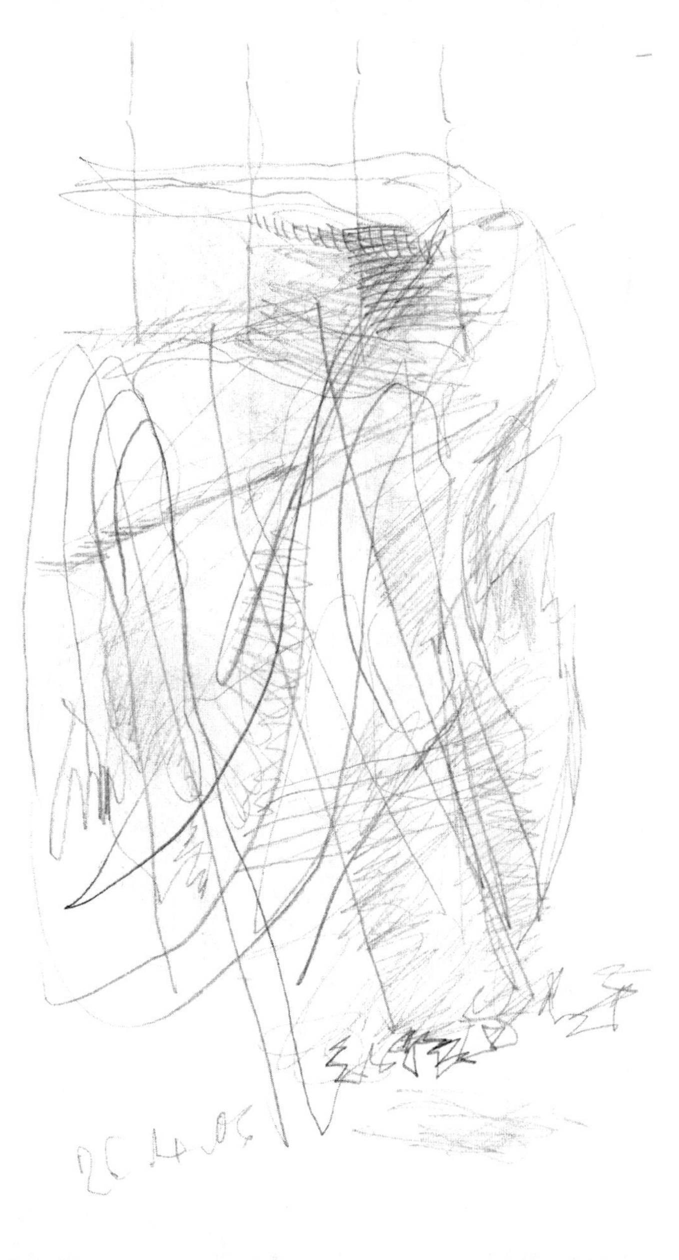

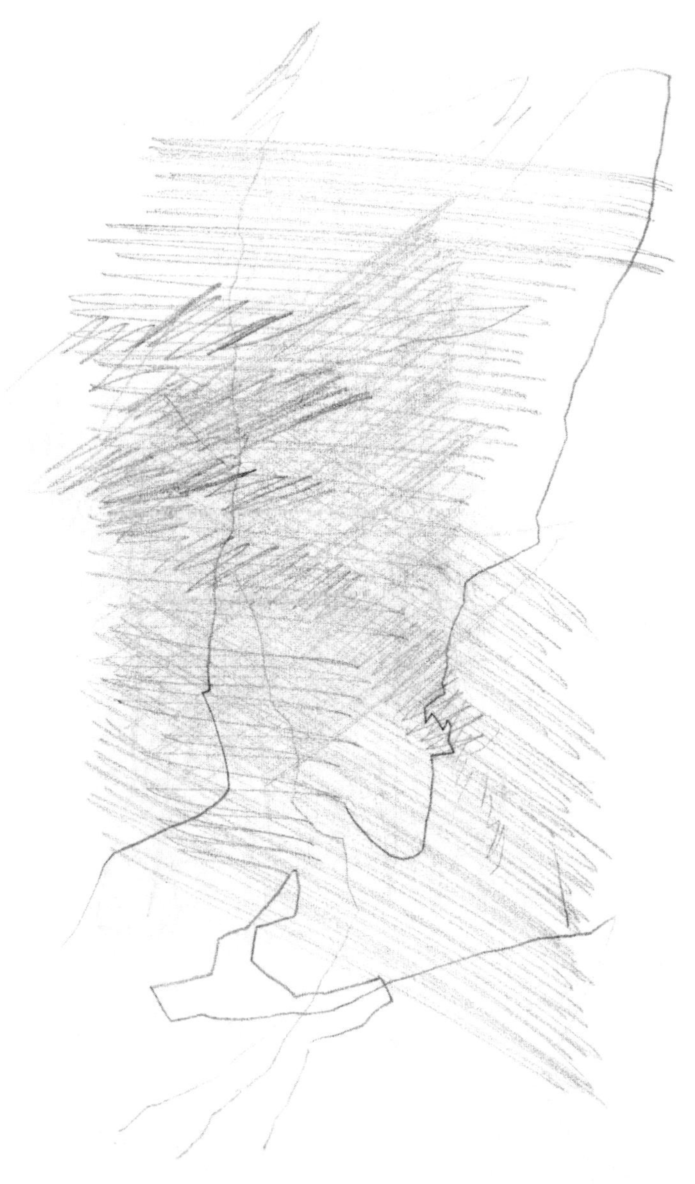

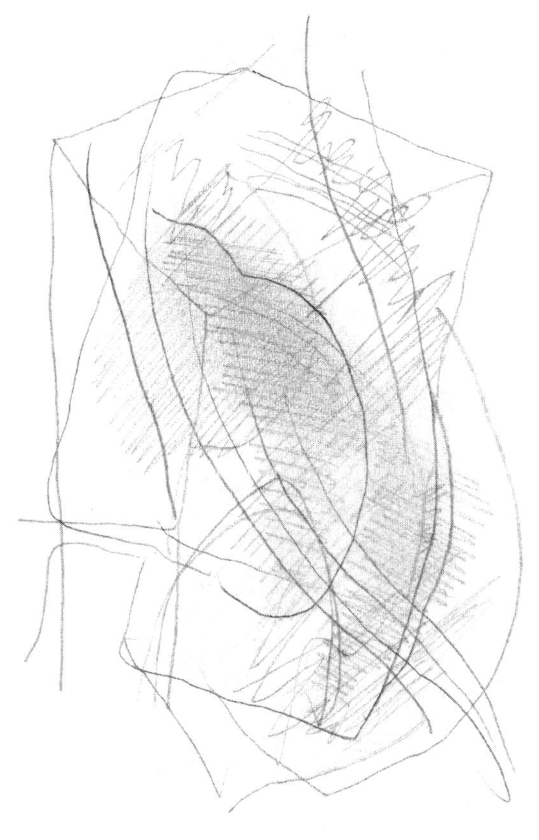

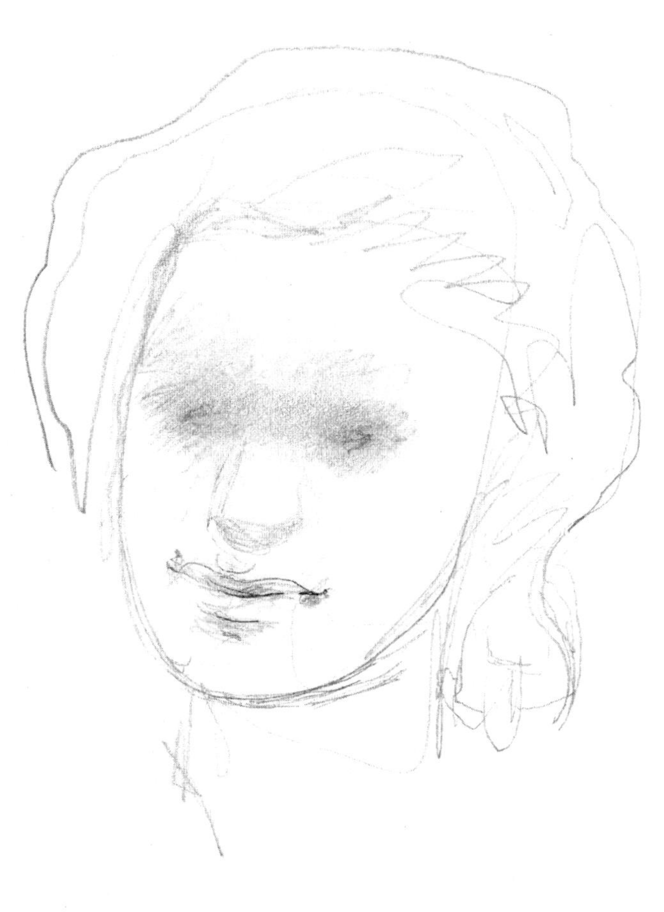

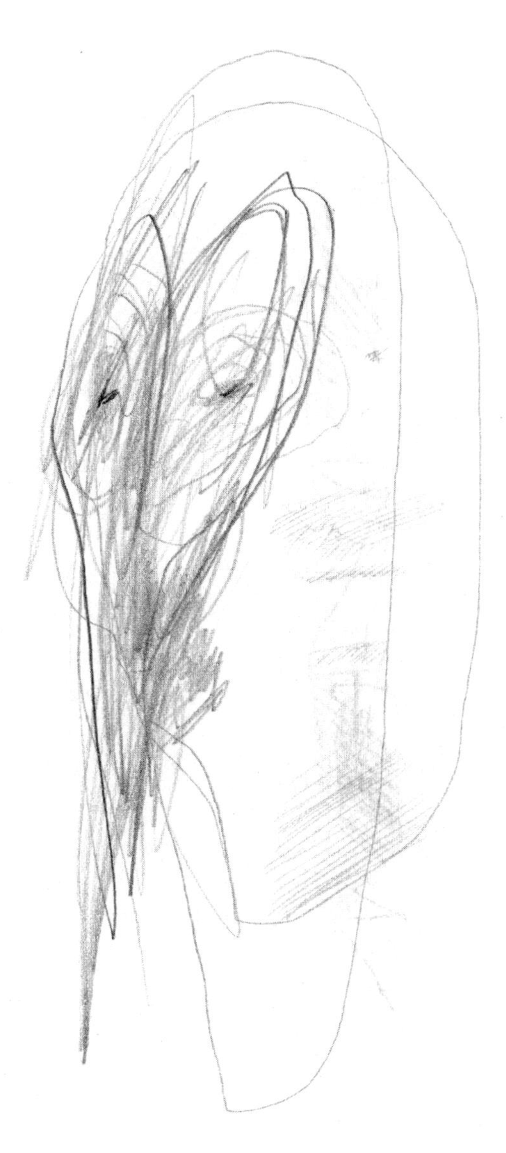

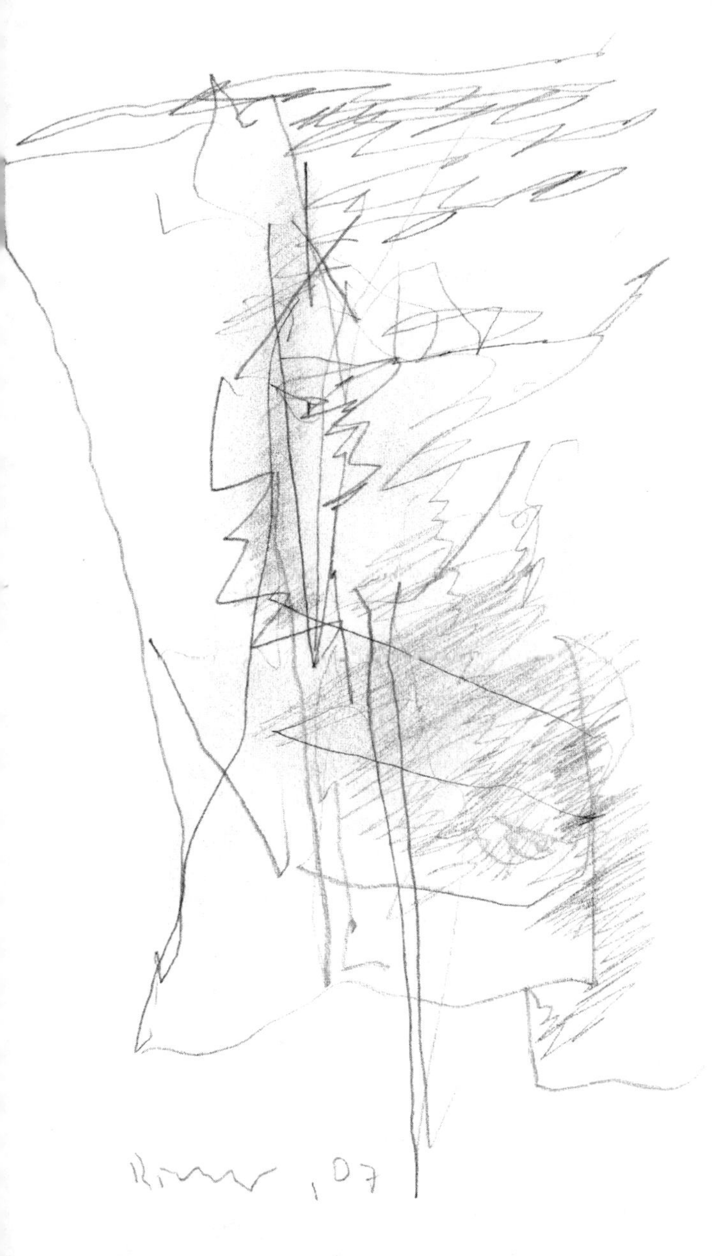

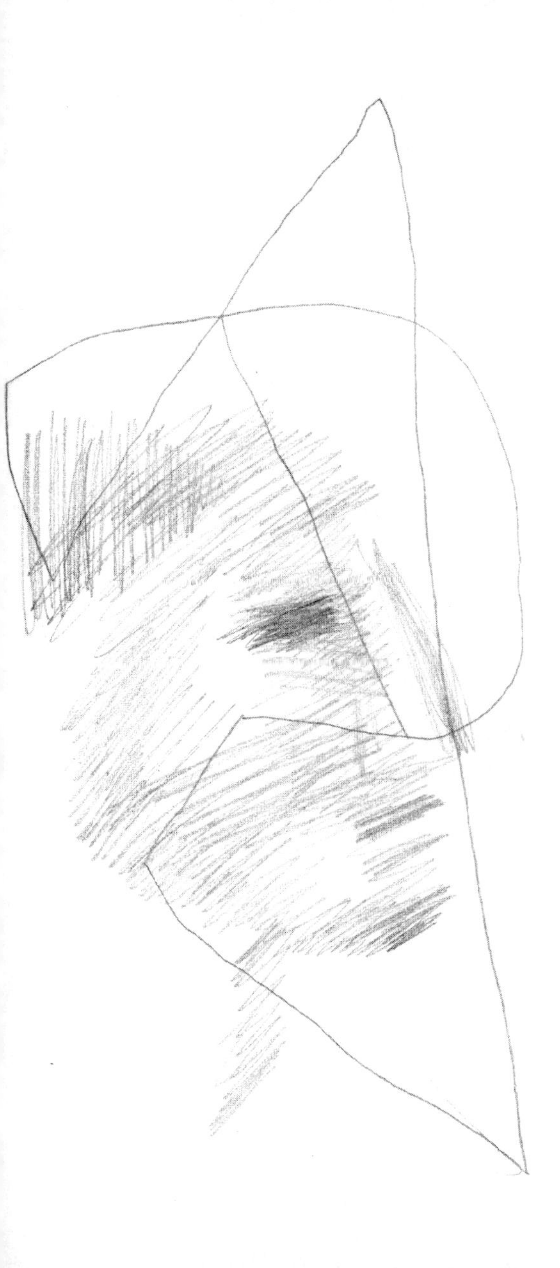

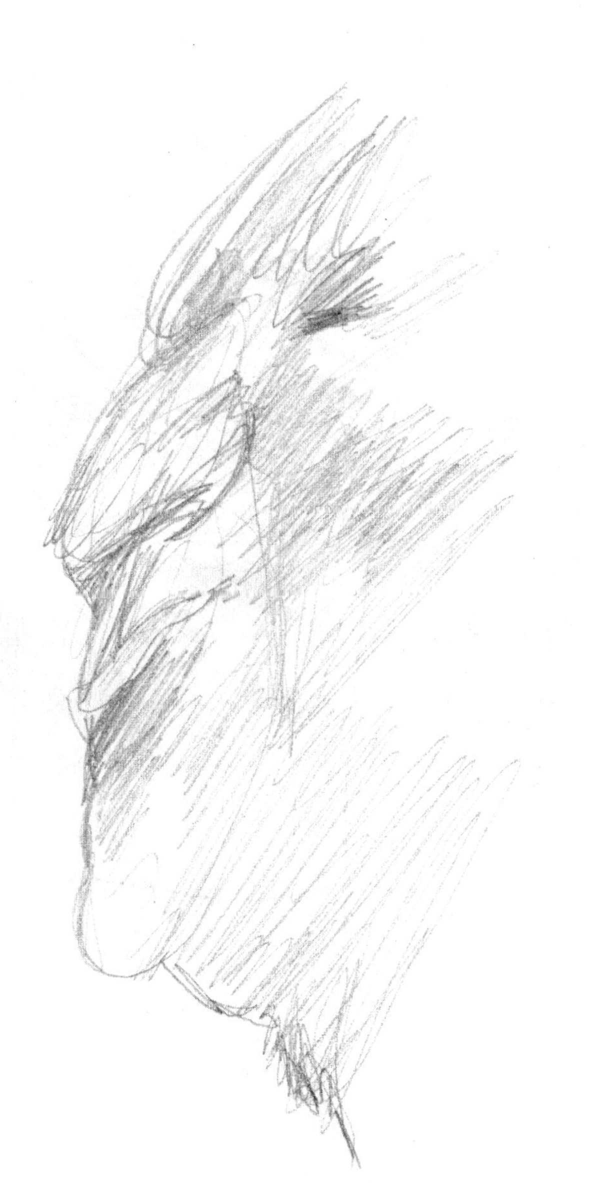

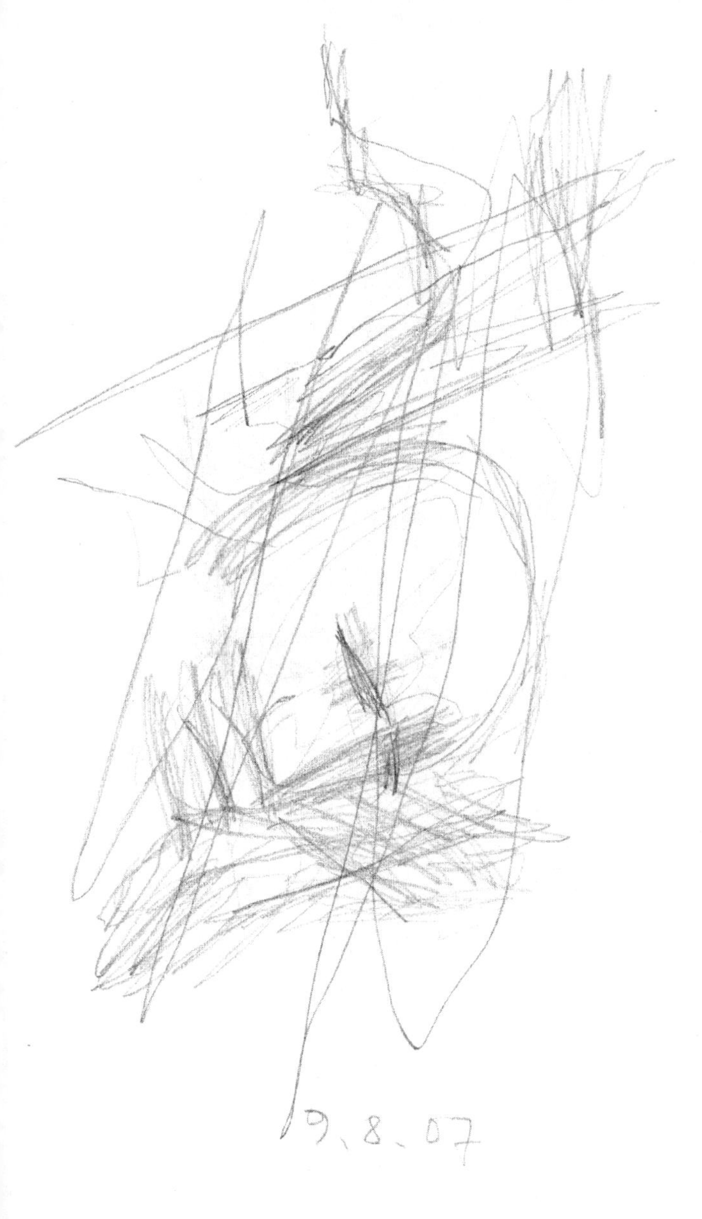
9.8.07

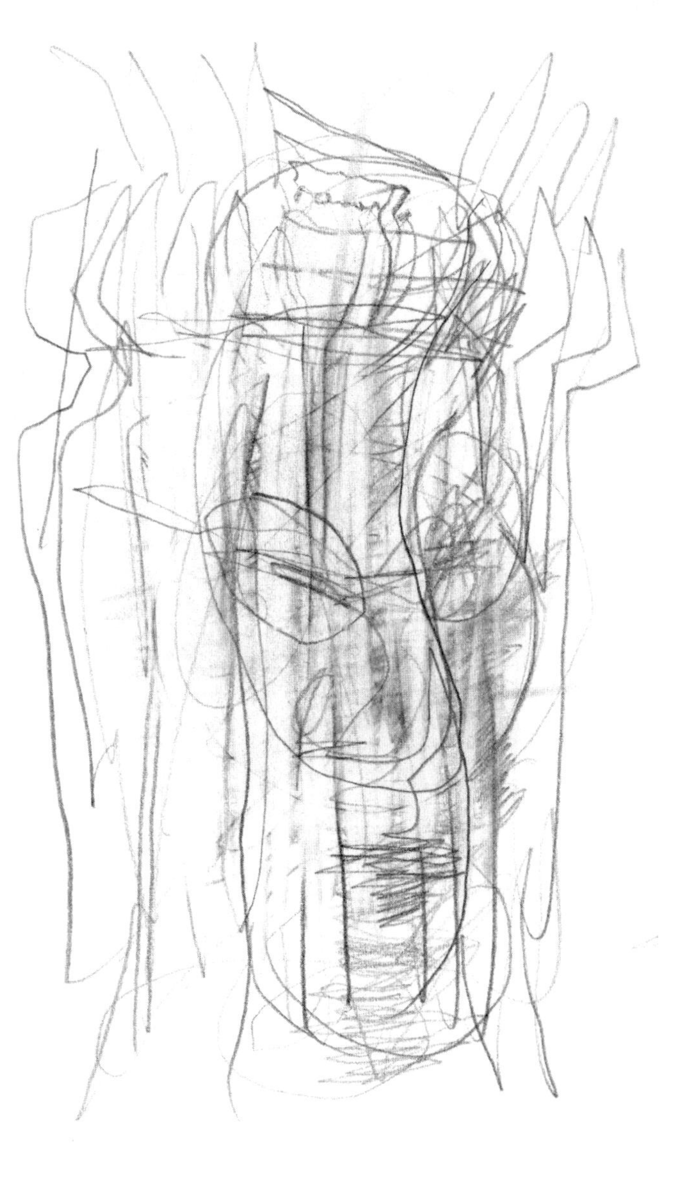

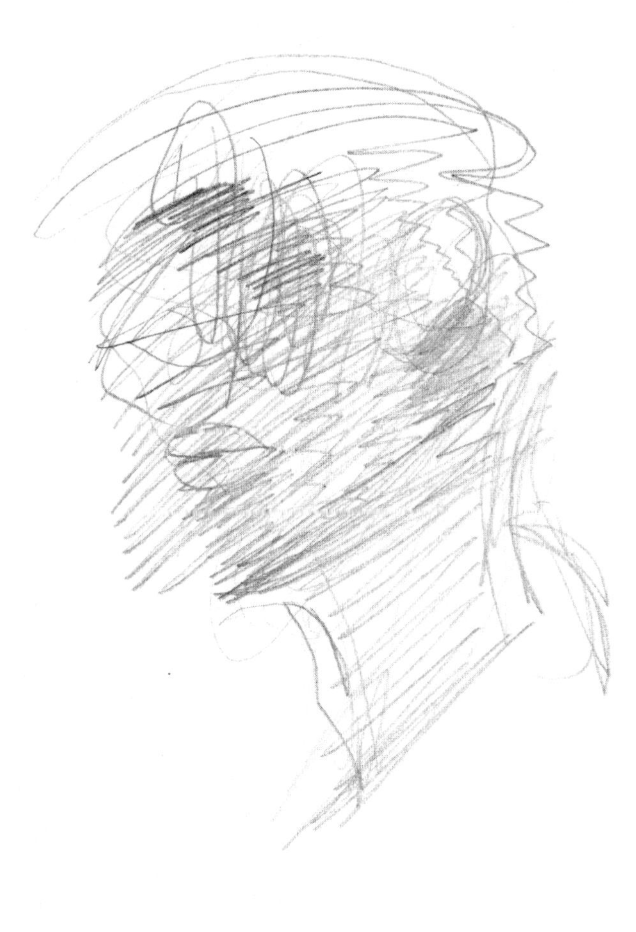

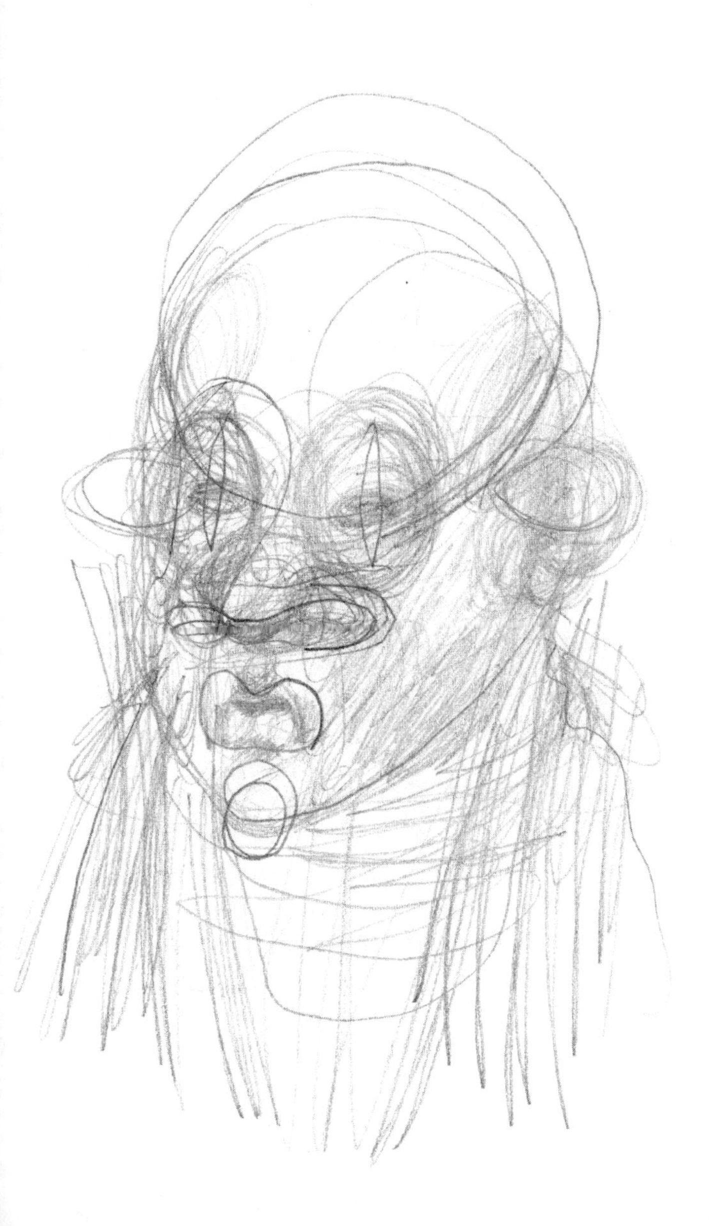

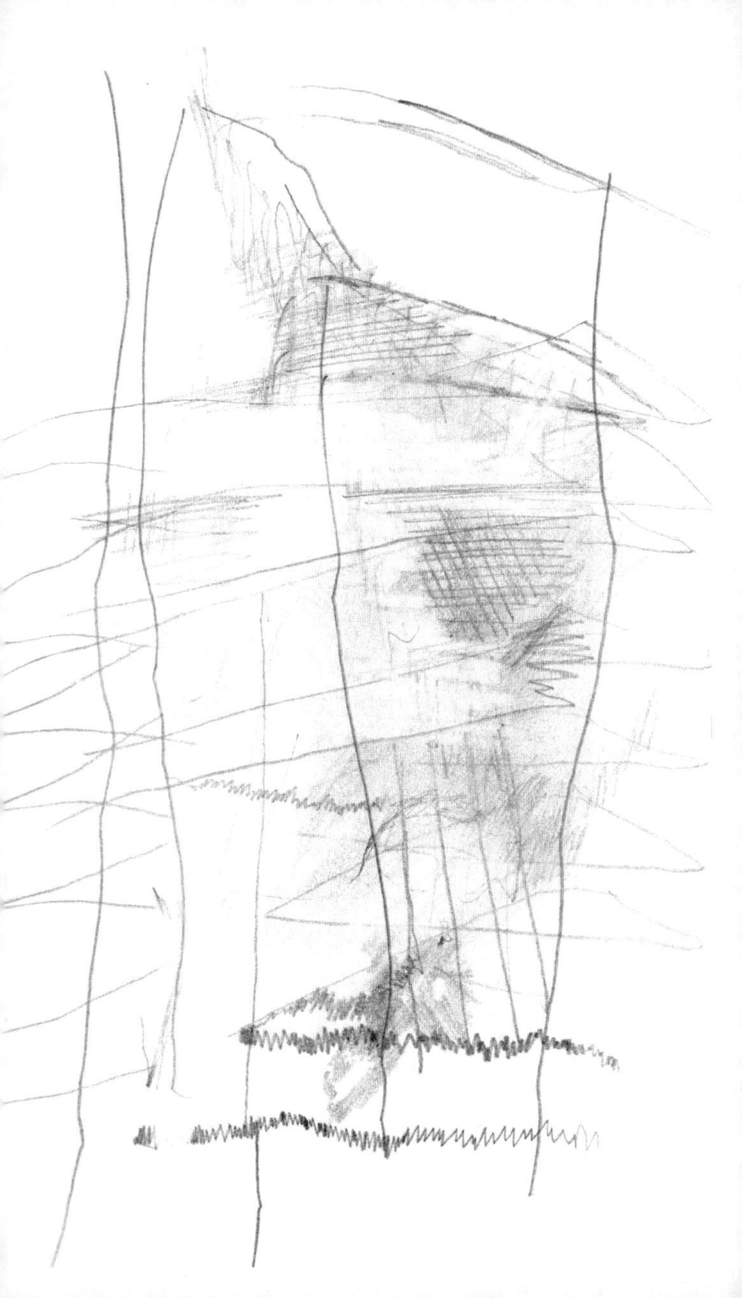

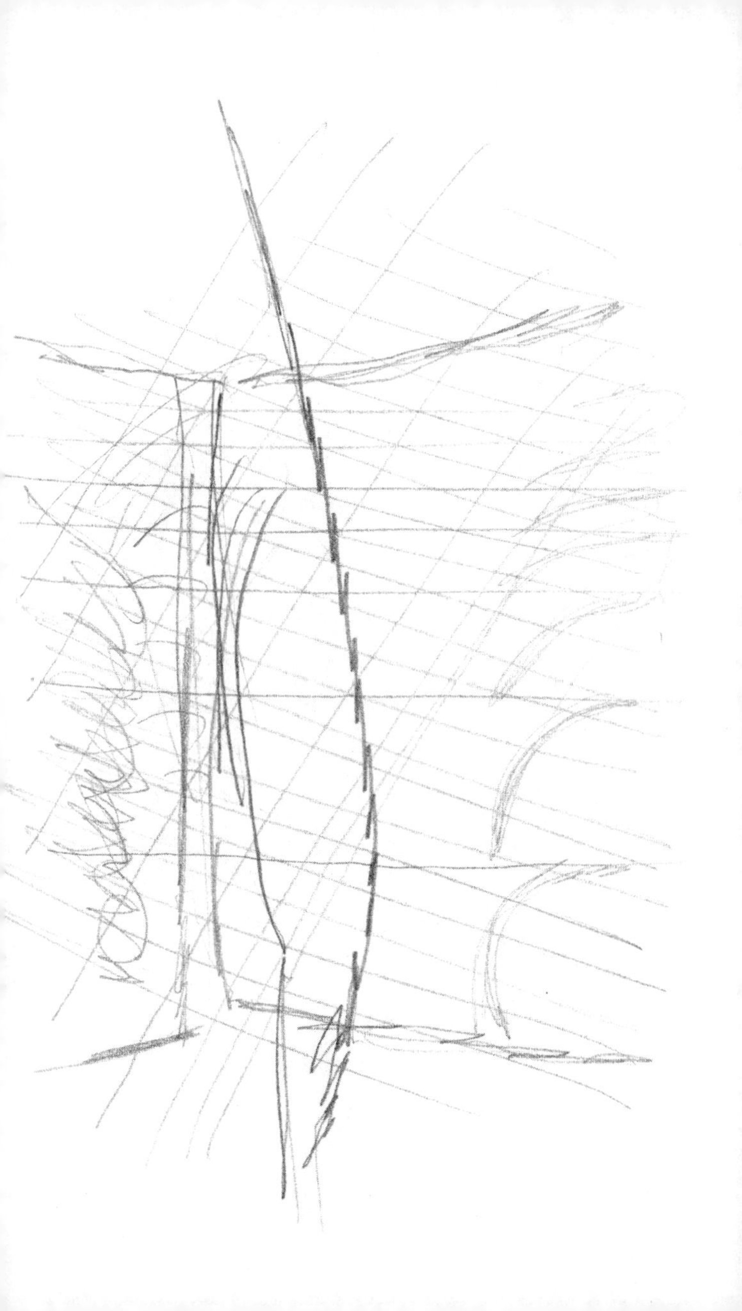

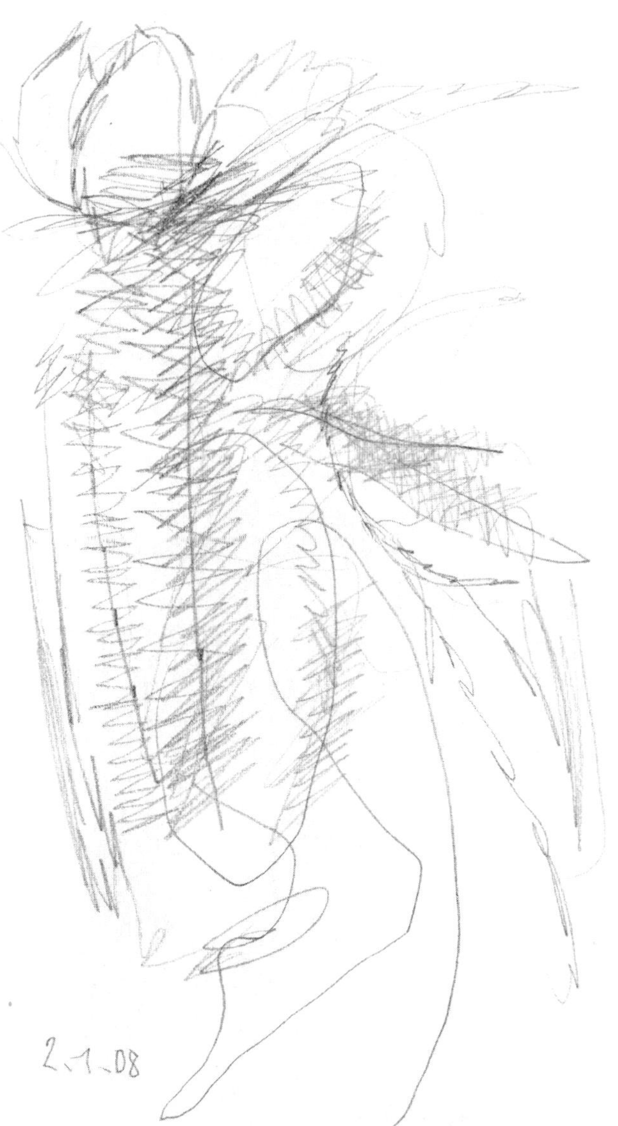
2.1.08

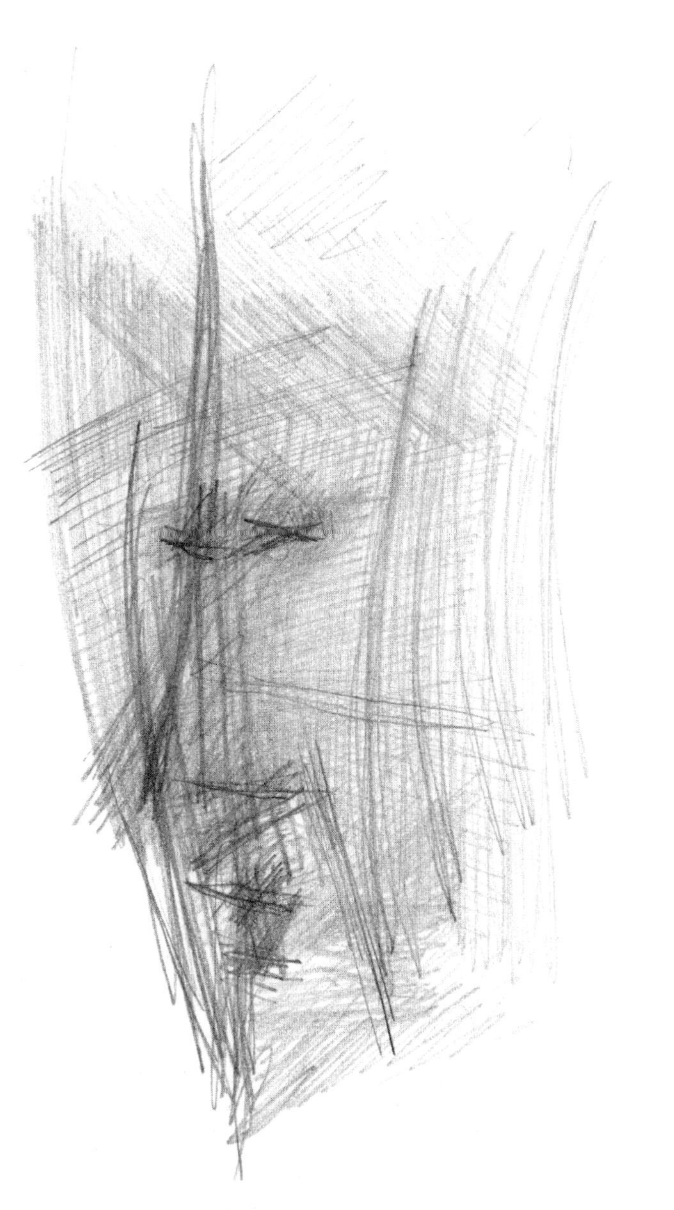

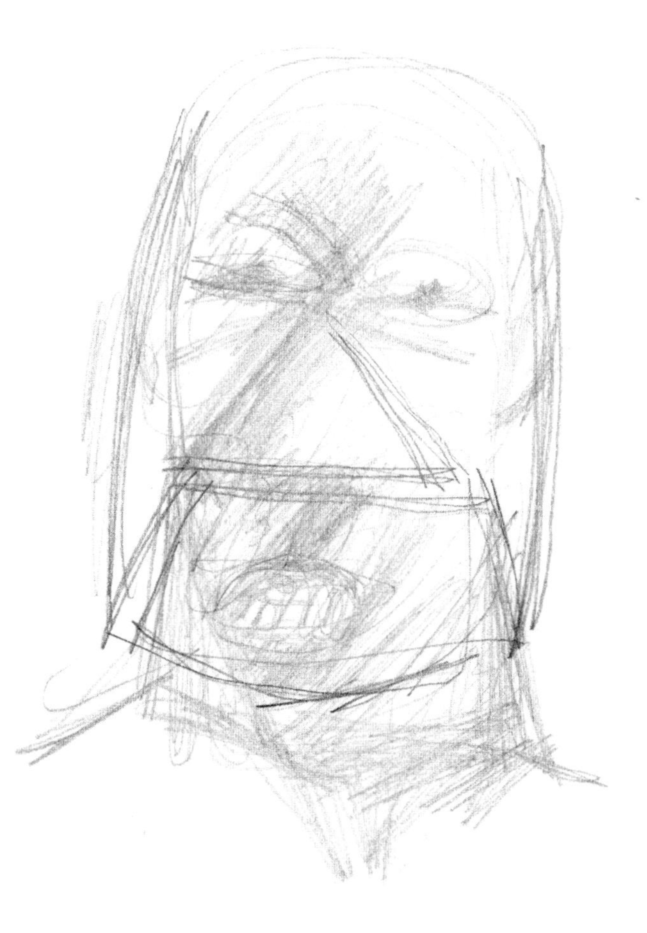

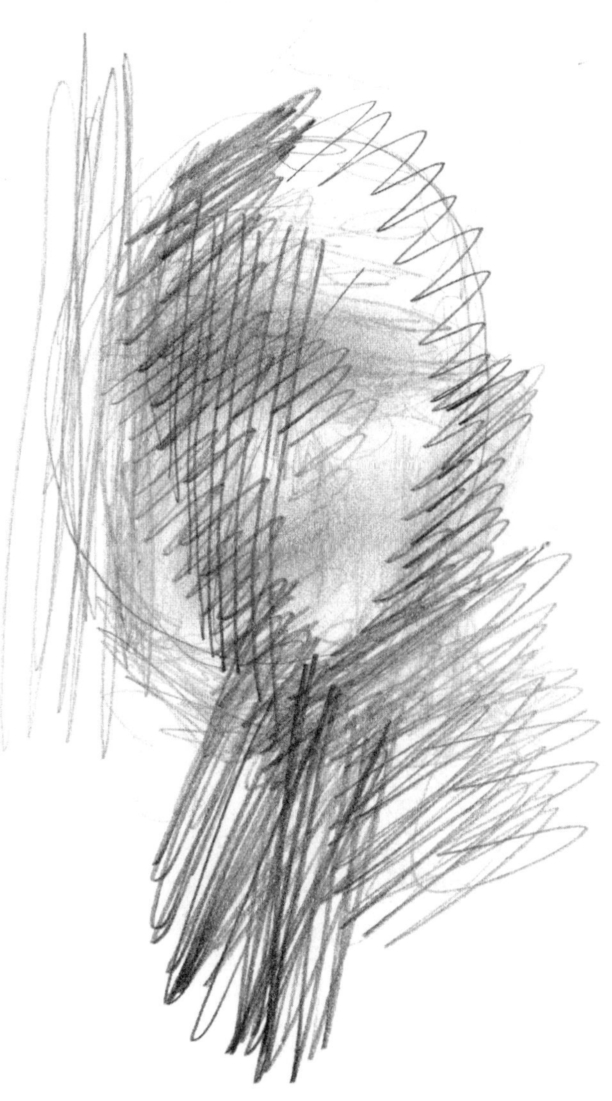

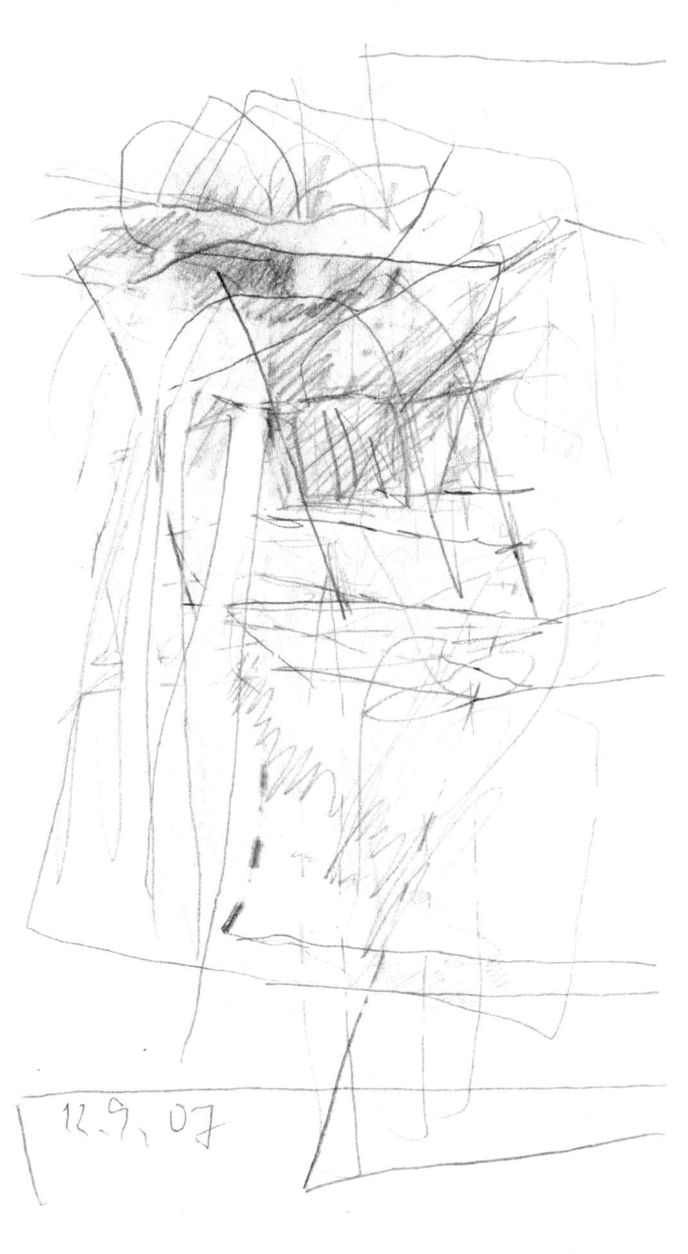
12.9.07

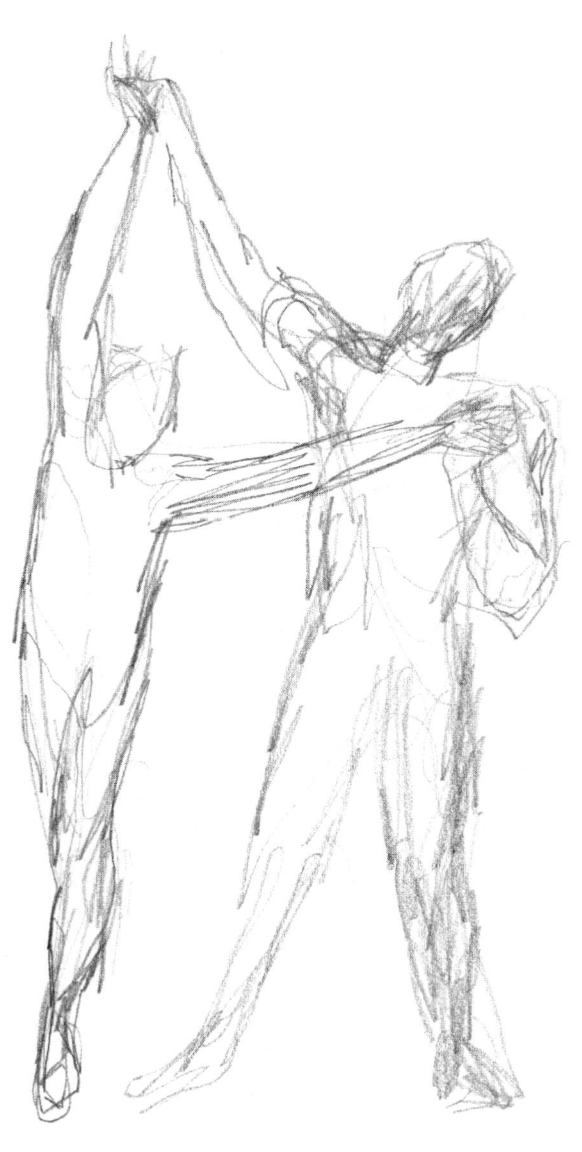

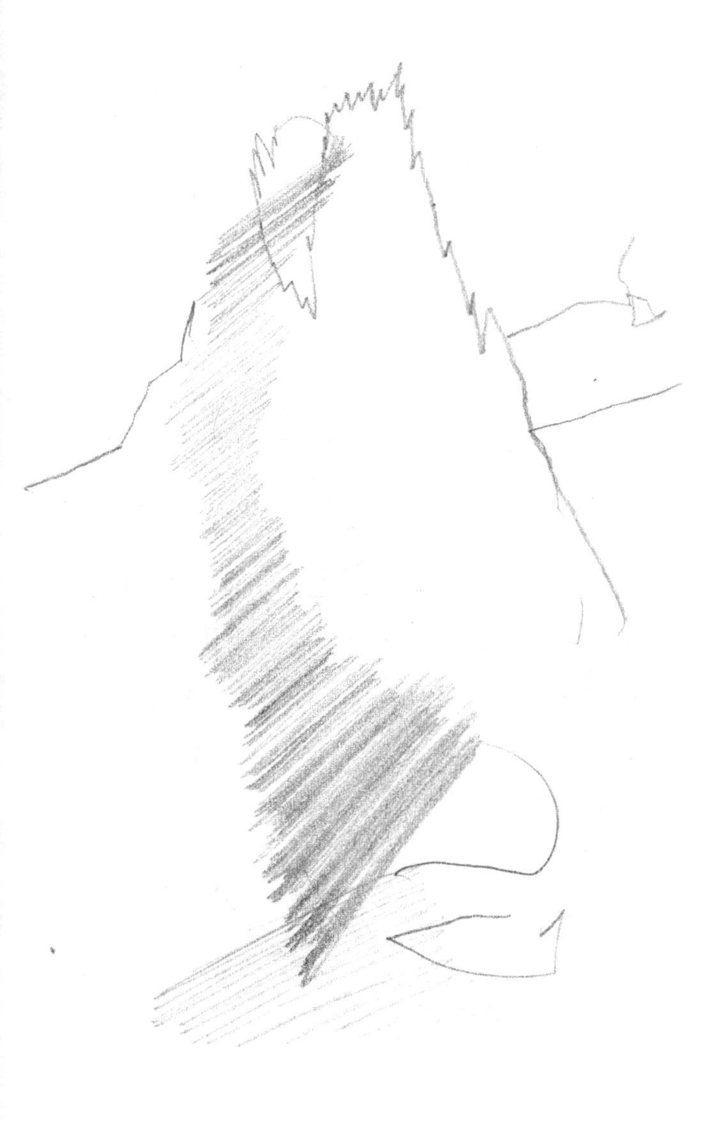

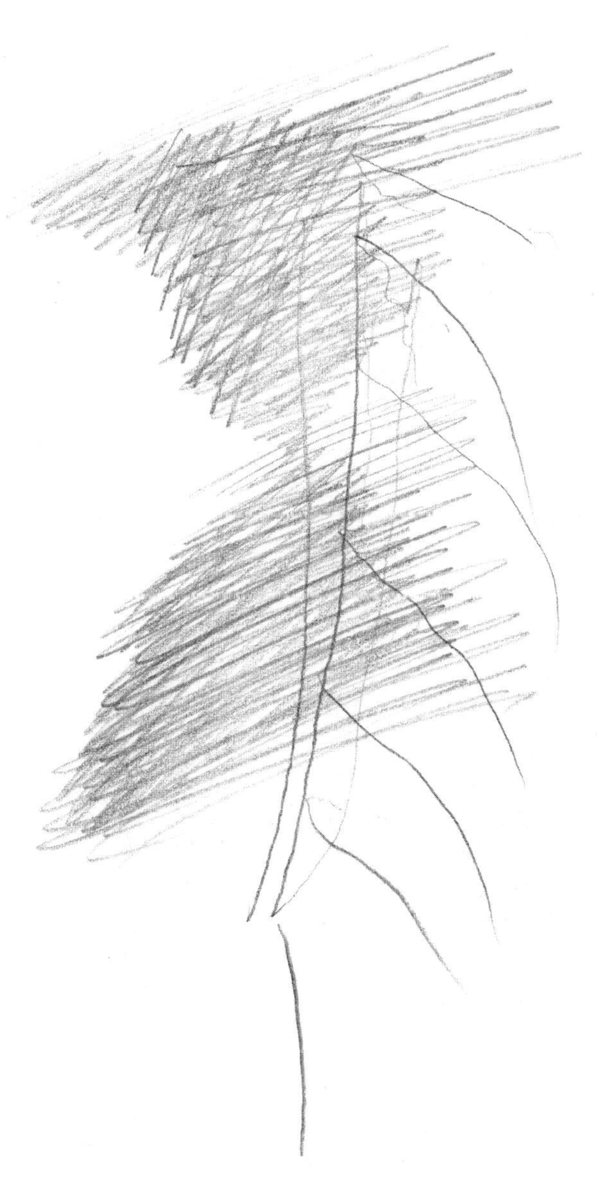

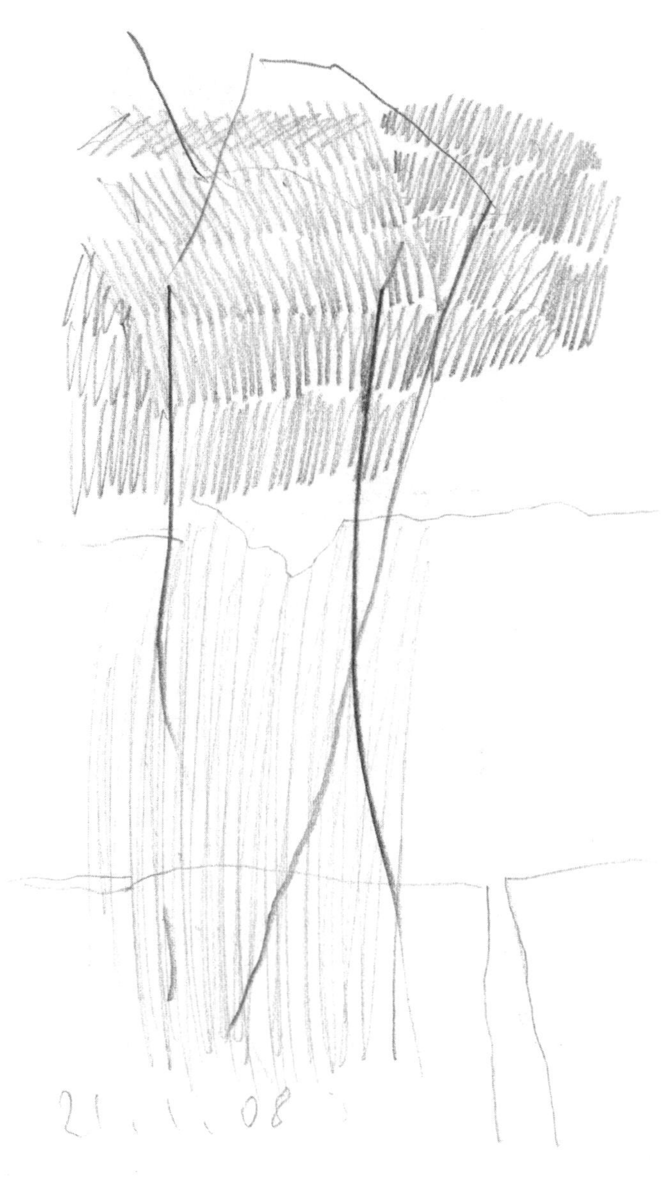
21.1.08

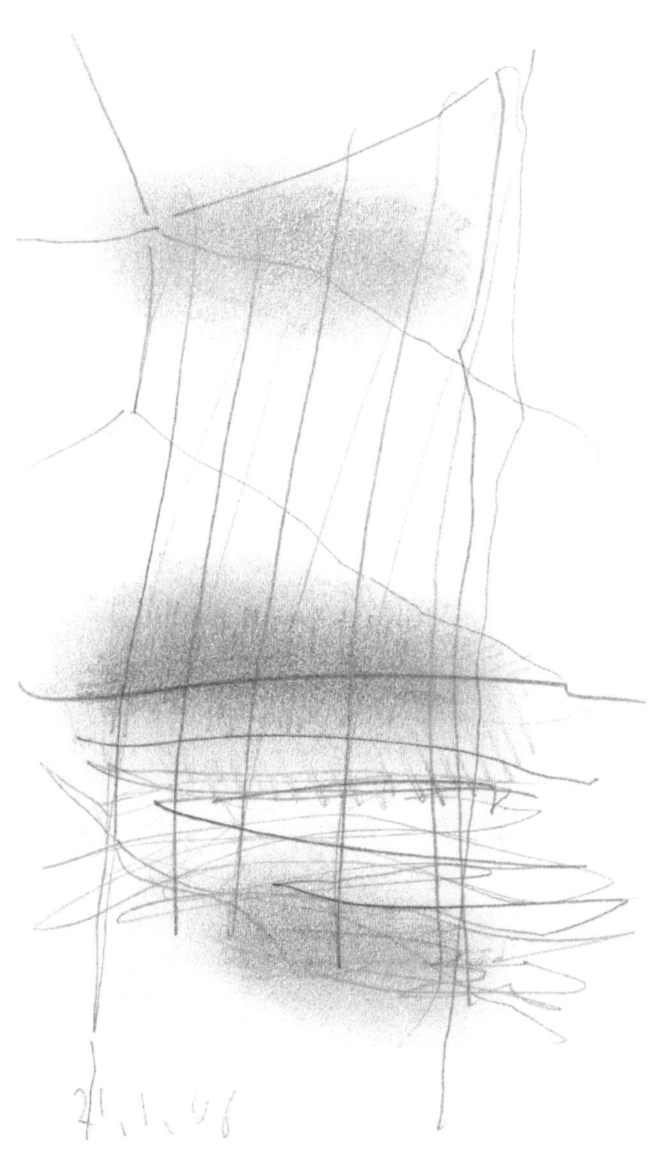
21.1.06

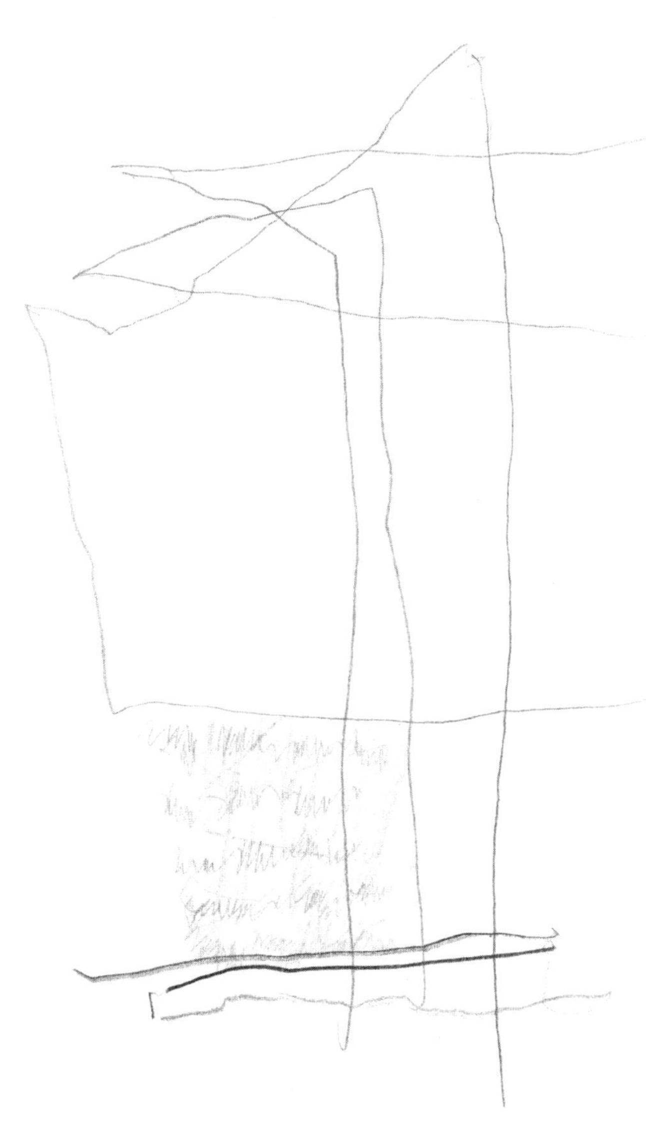

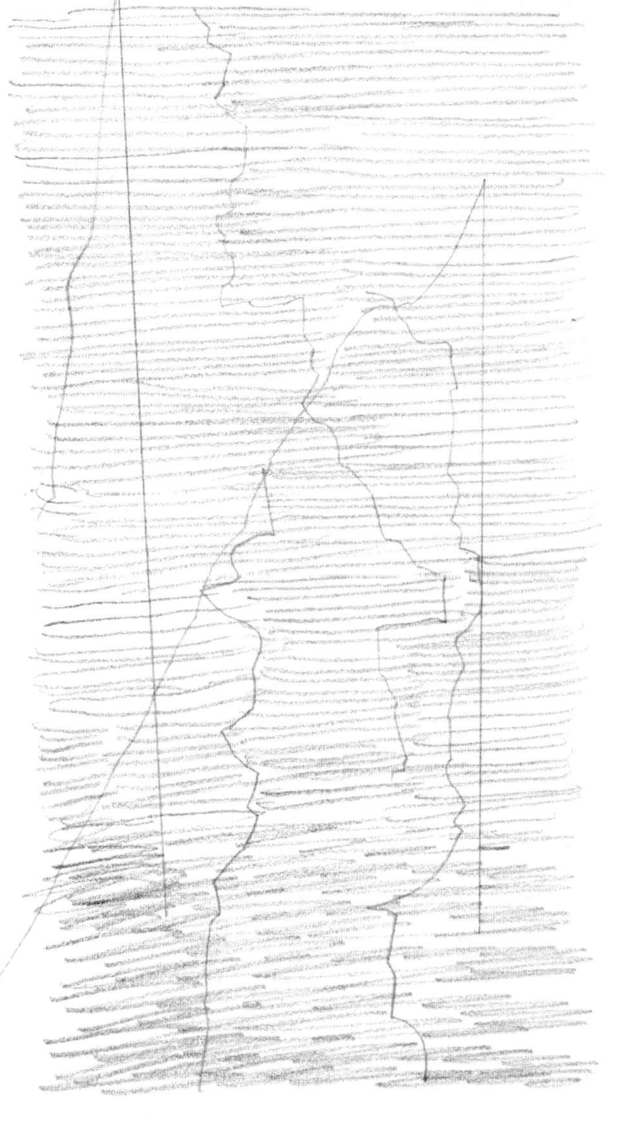

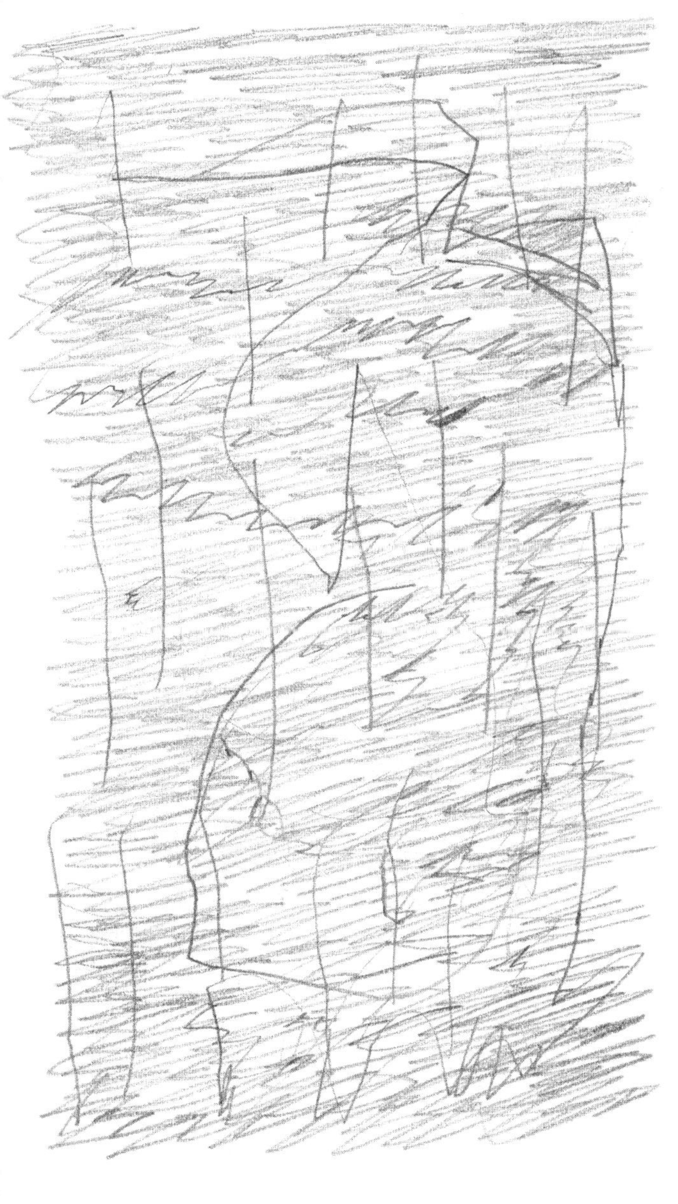

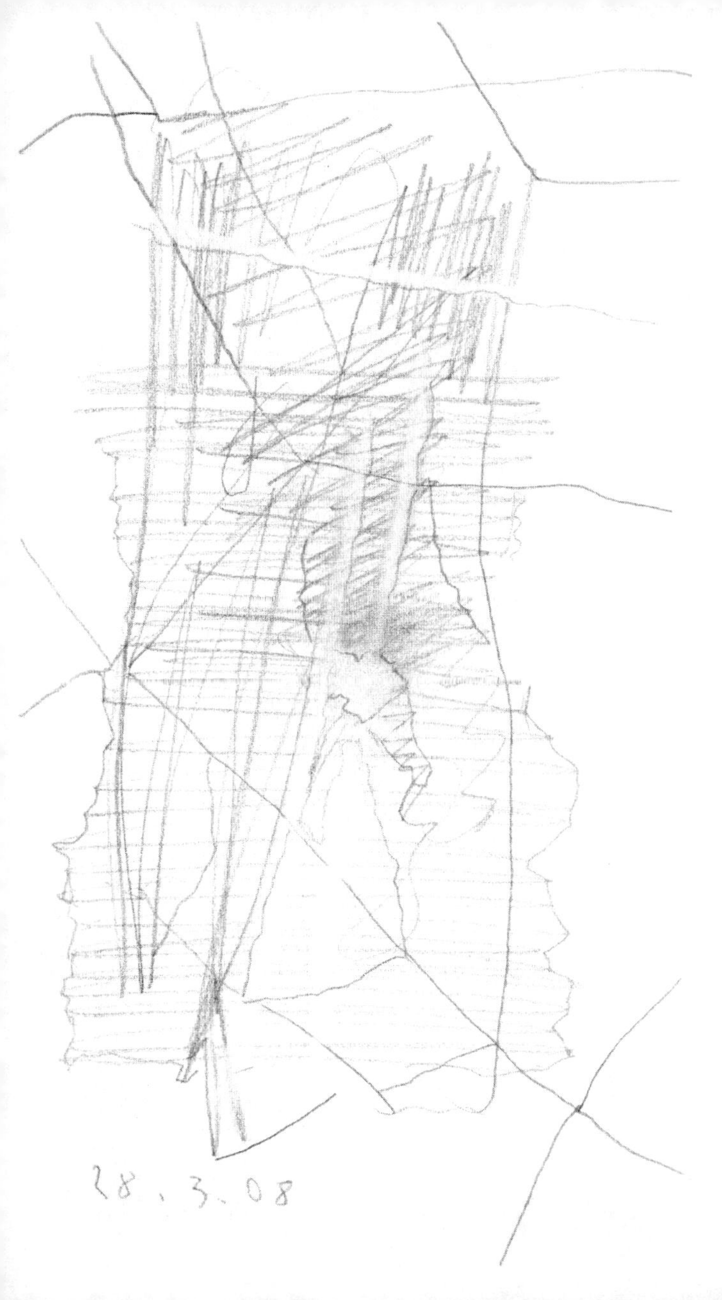
28.3.08

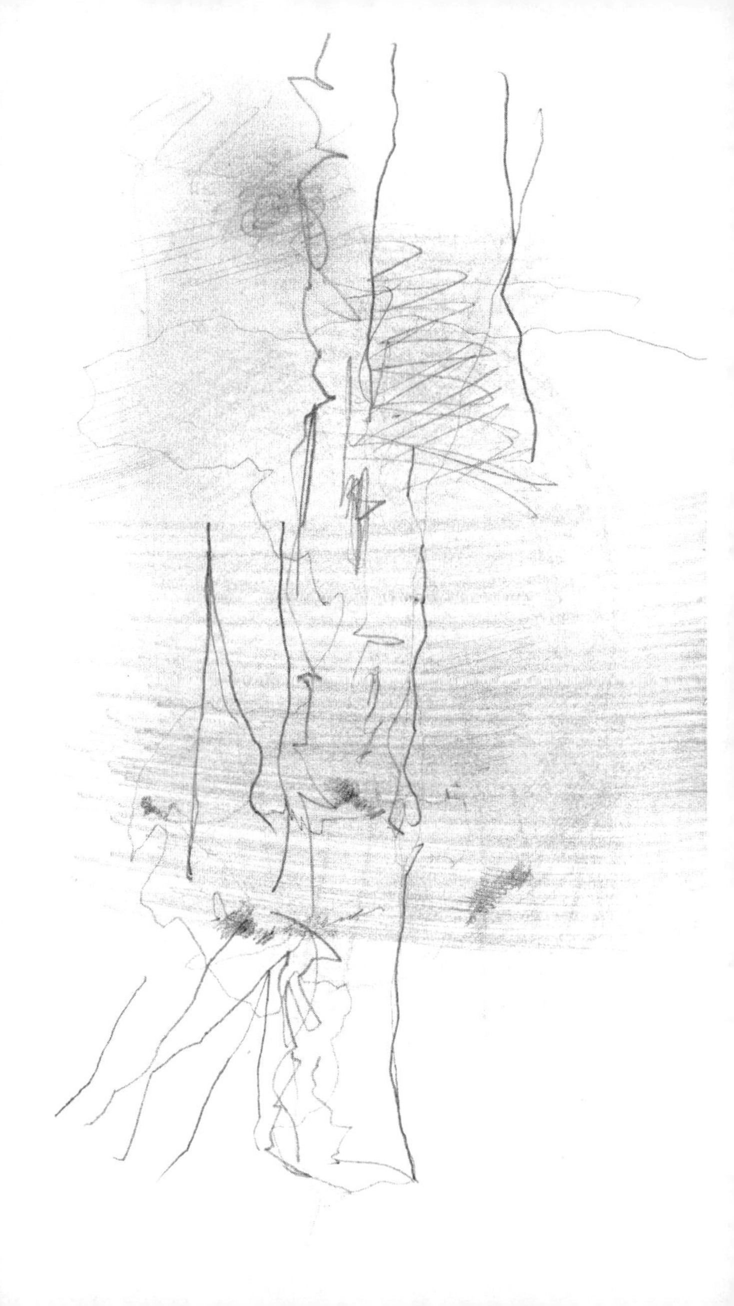

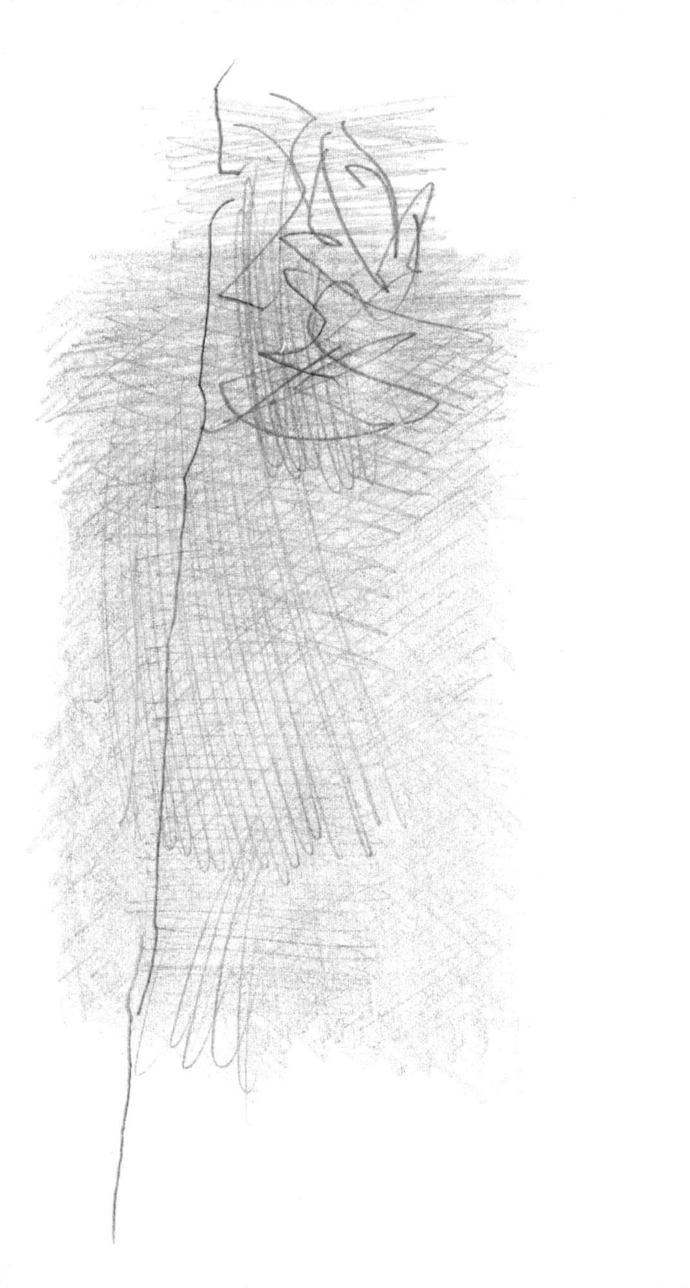

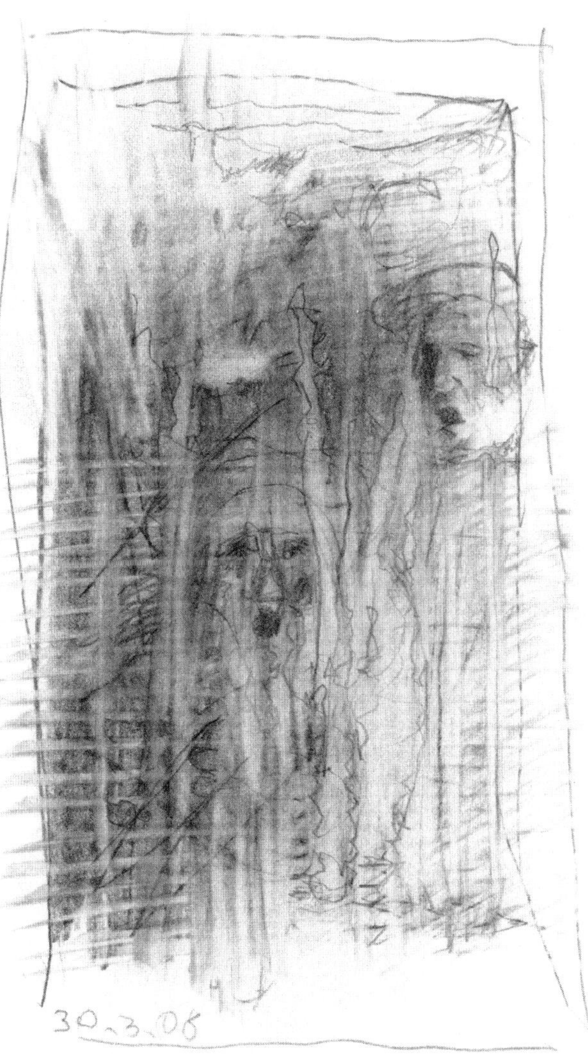
30.3.06

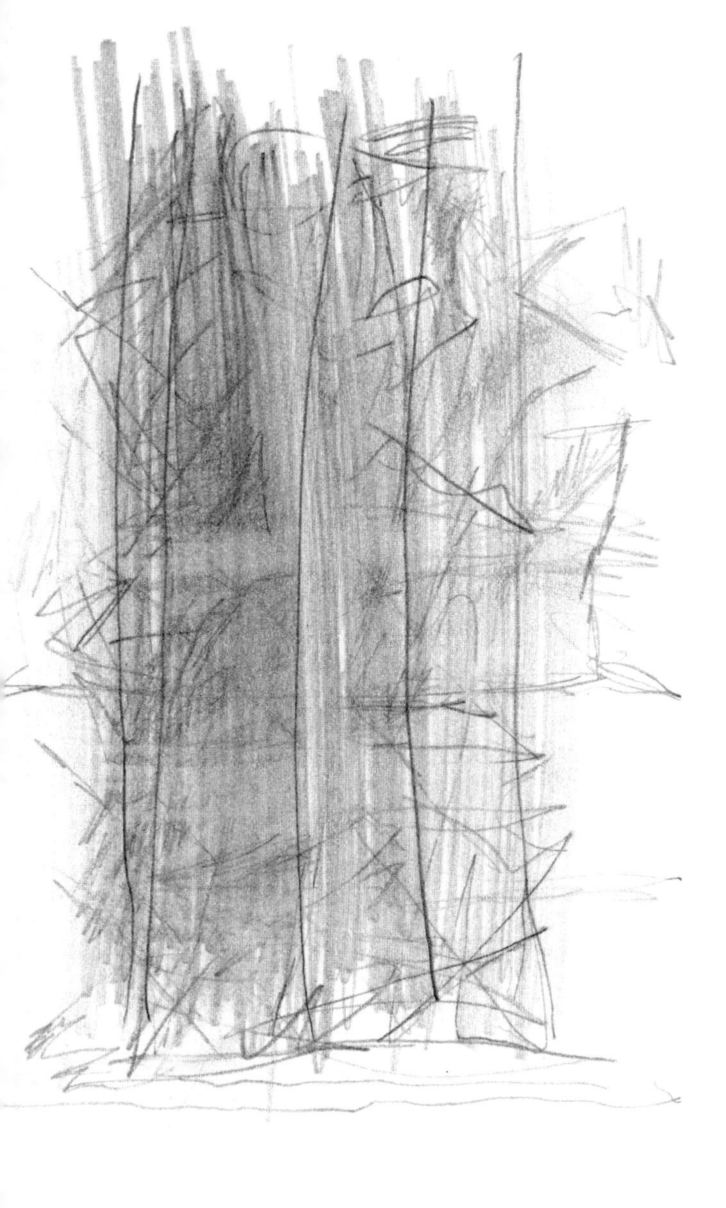

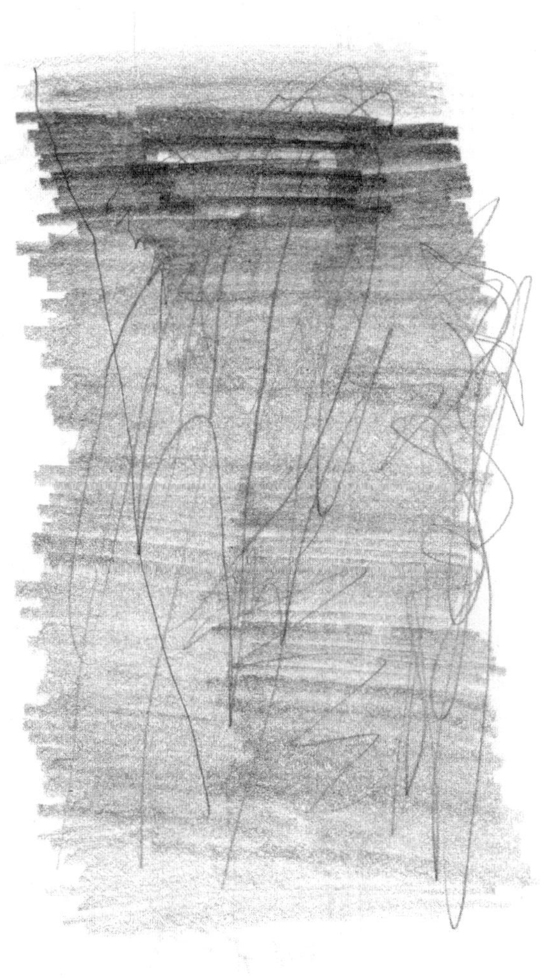

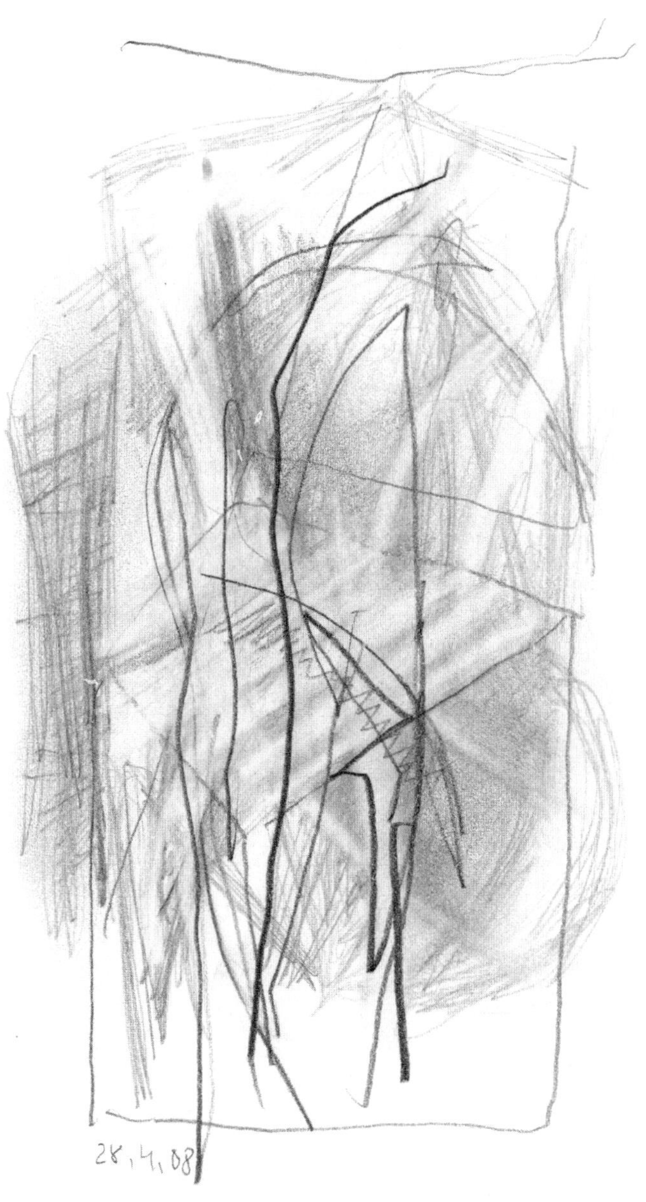
28.4.08

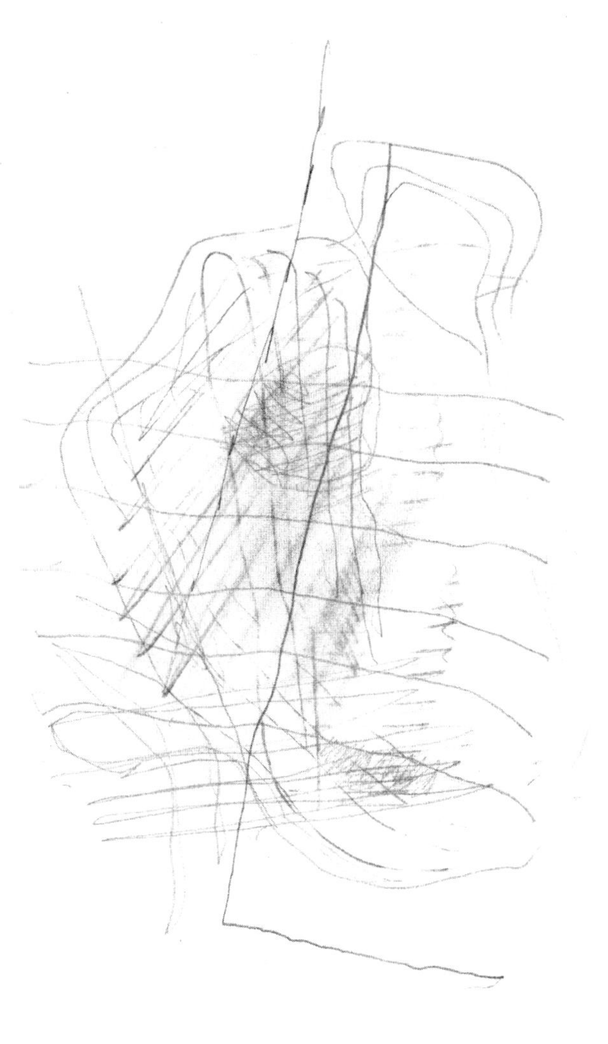

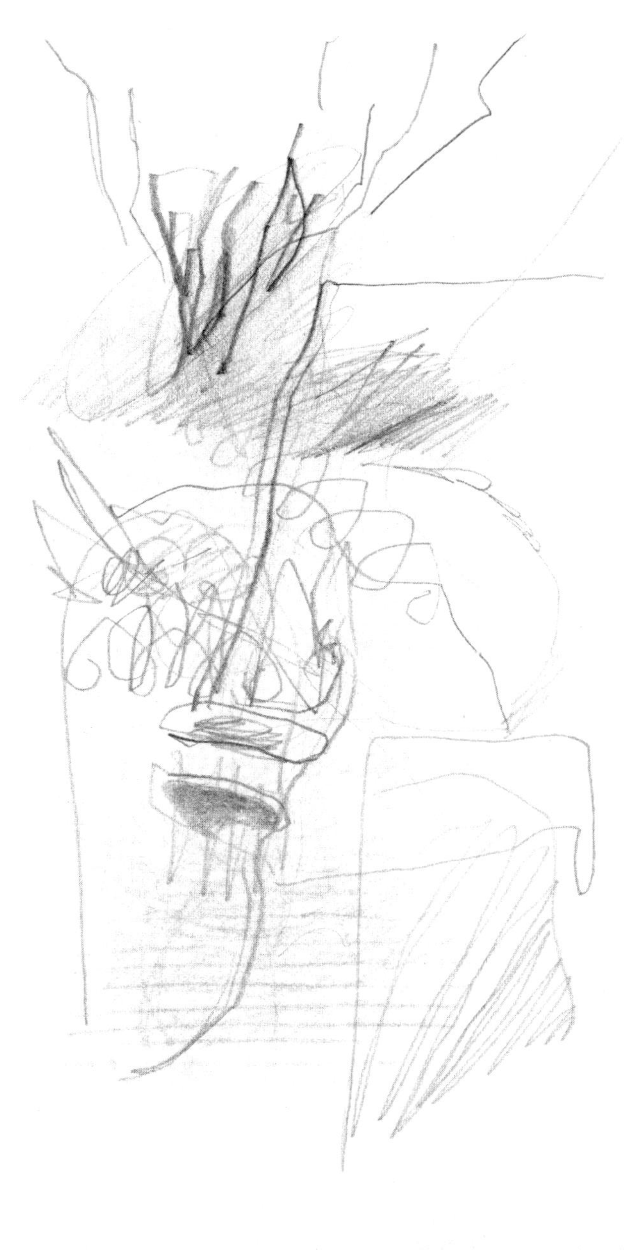

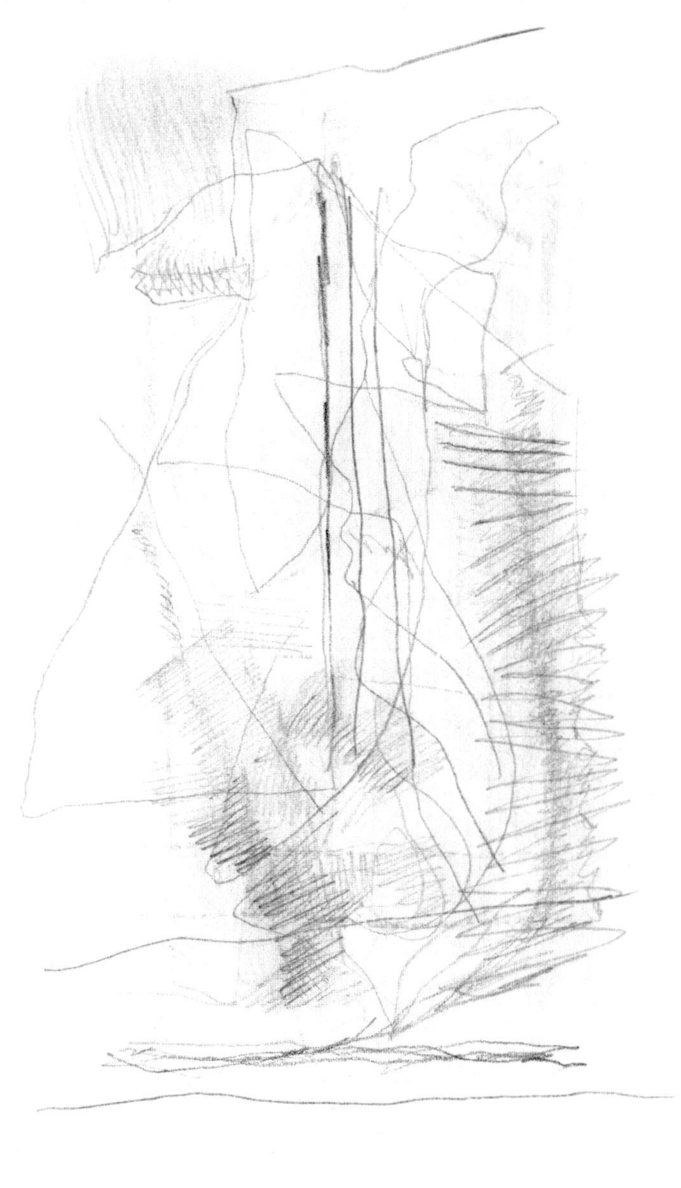

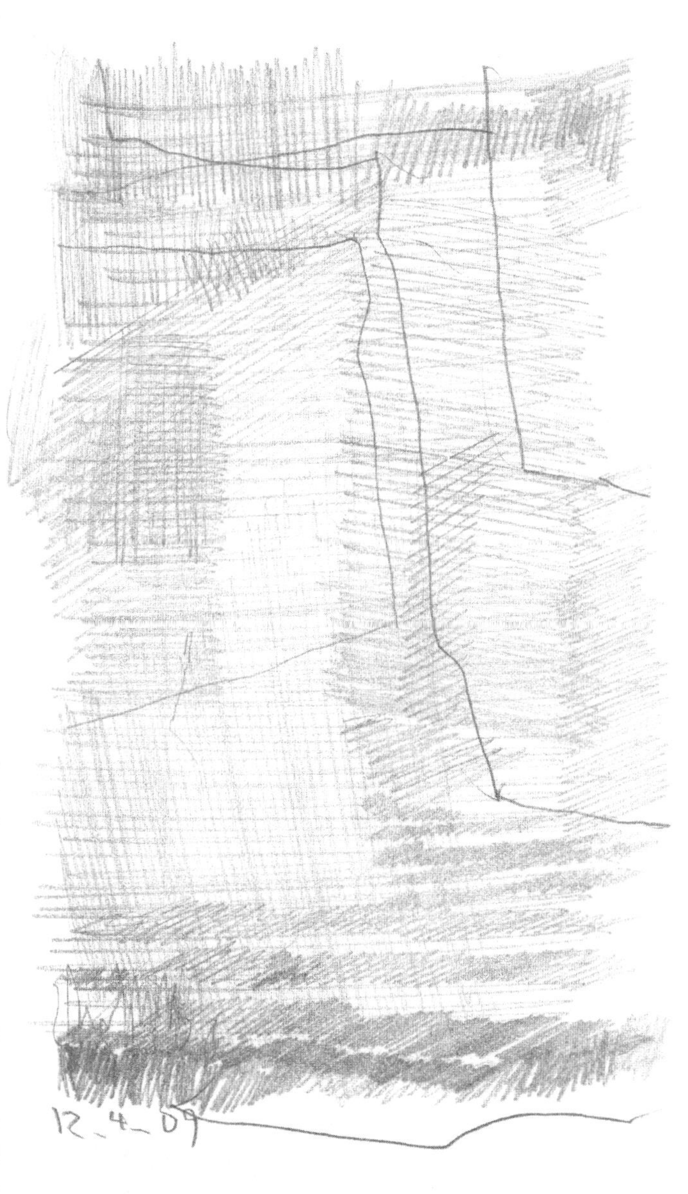
12_4_09

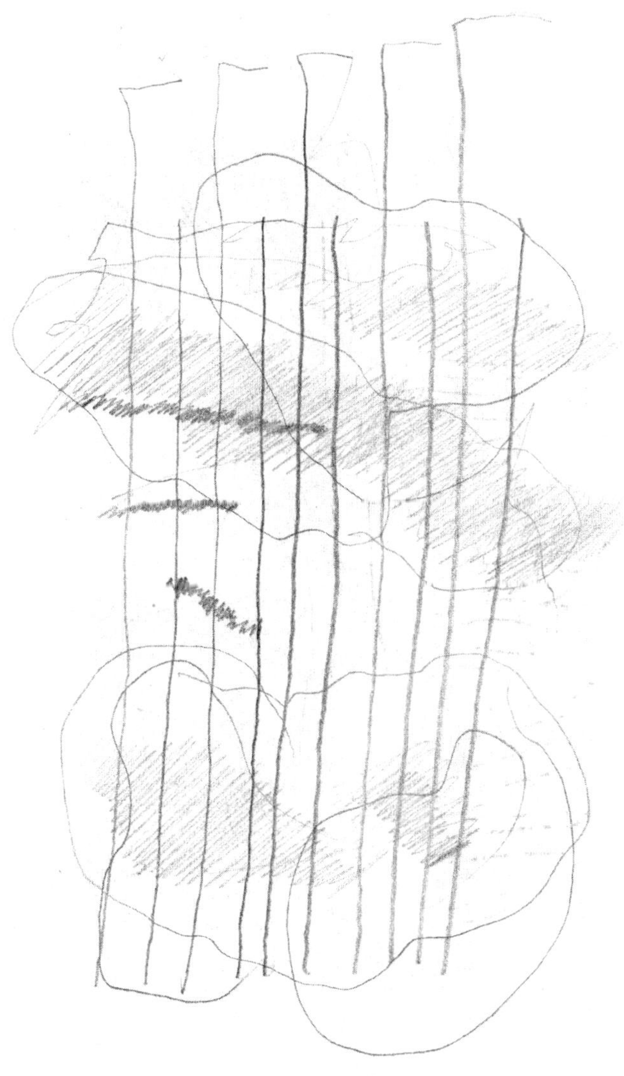

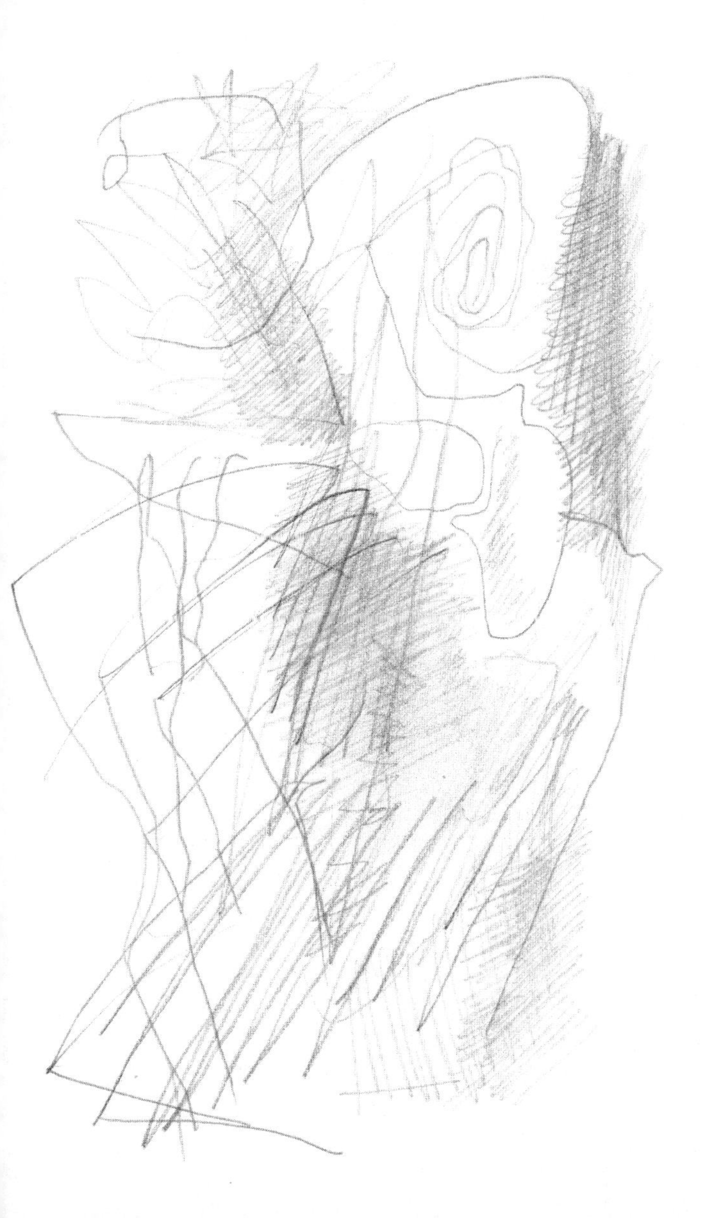

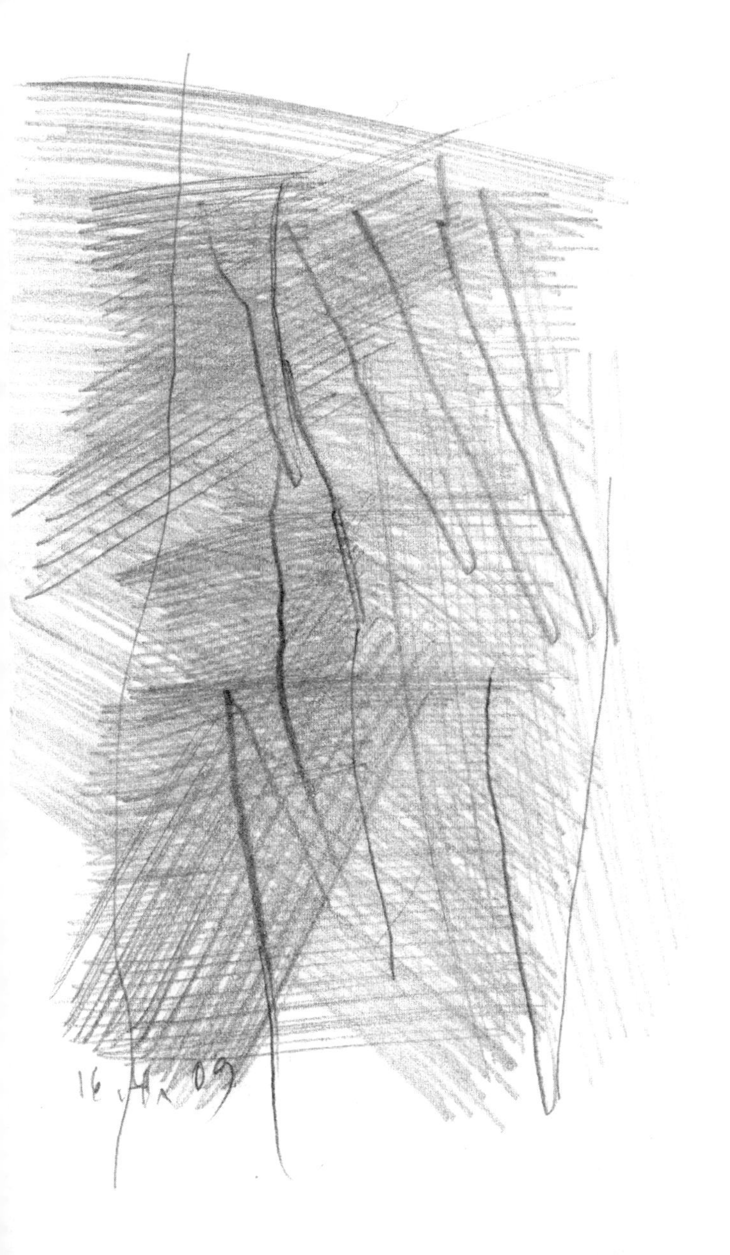

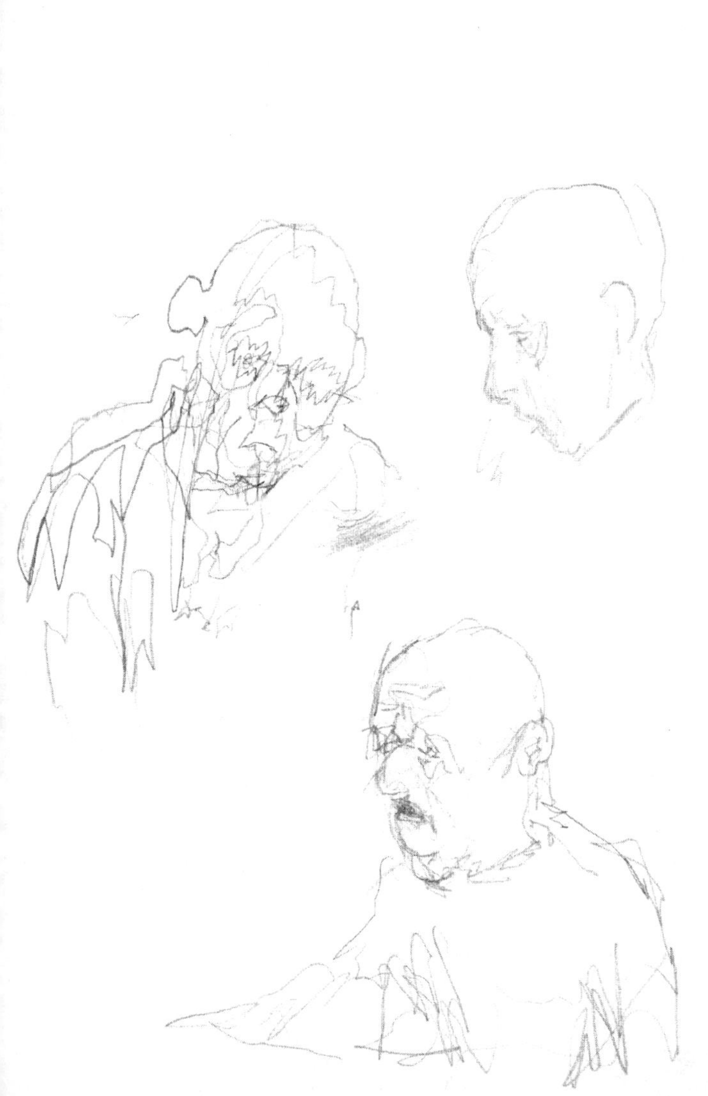

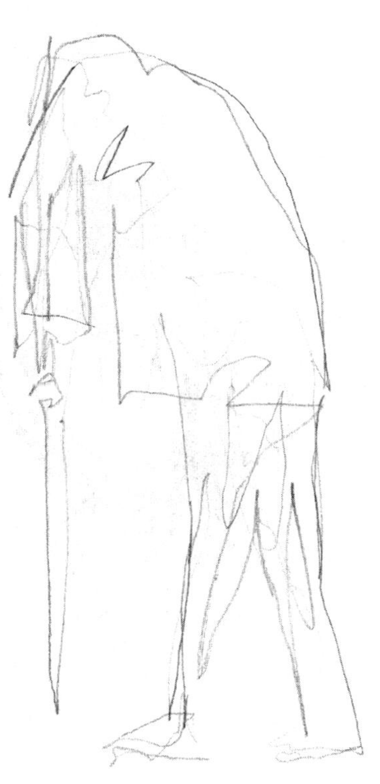

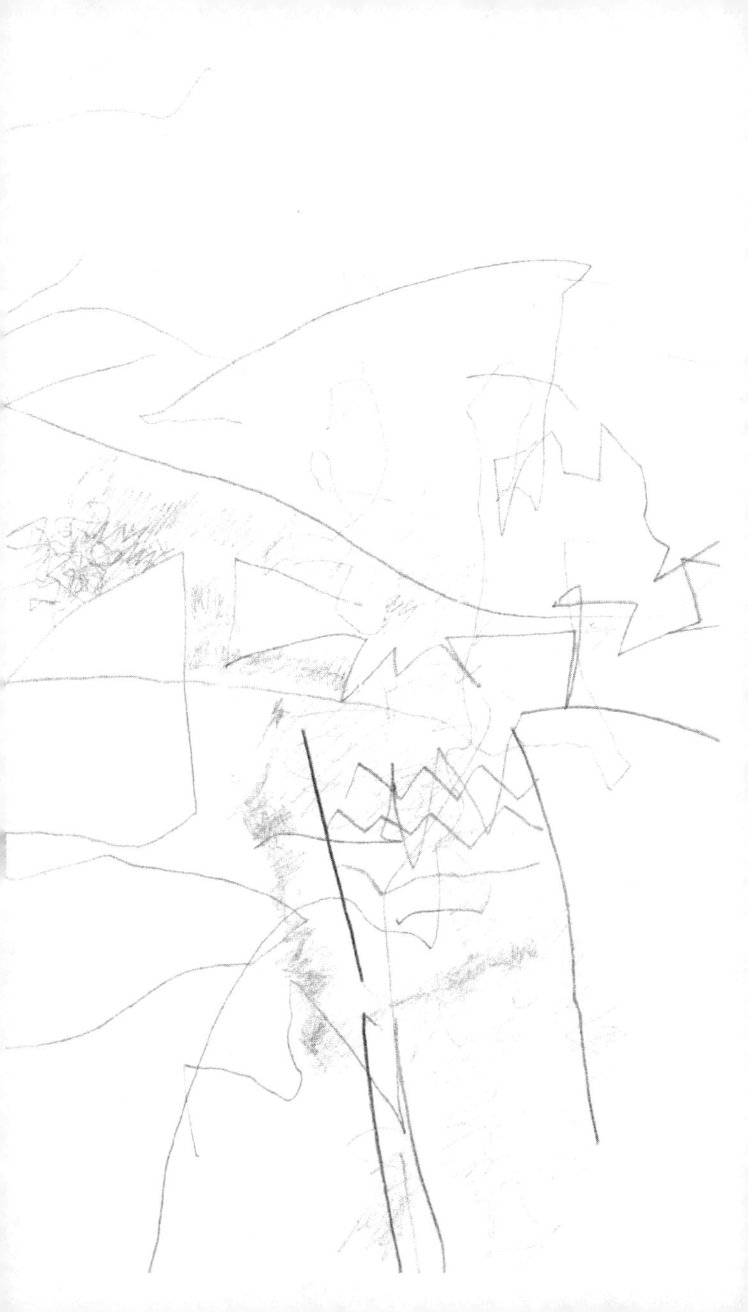

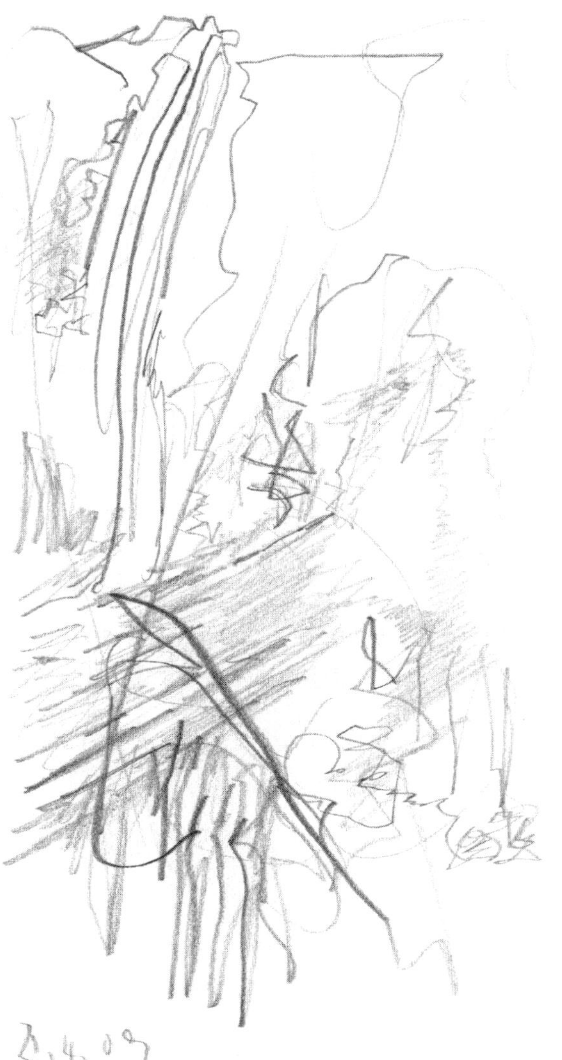

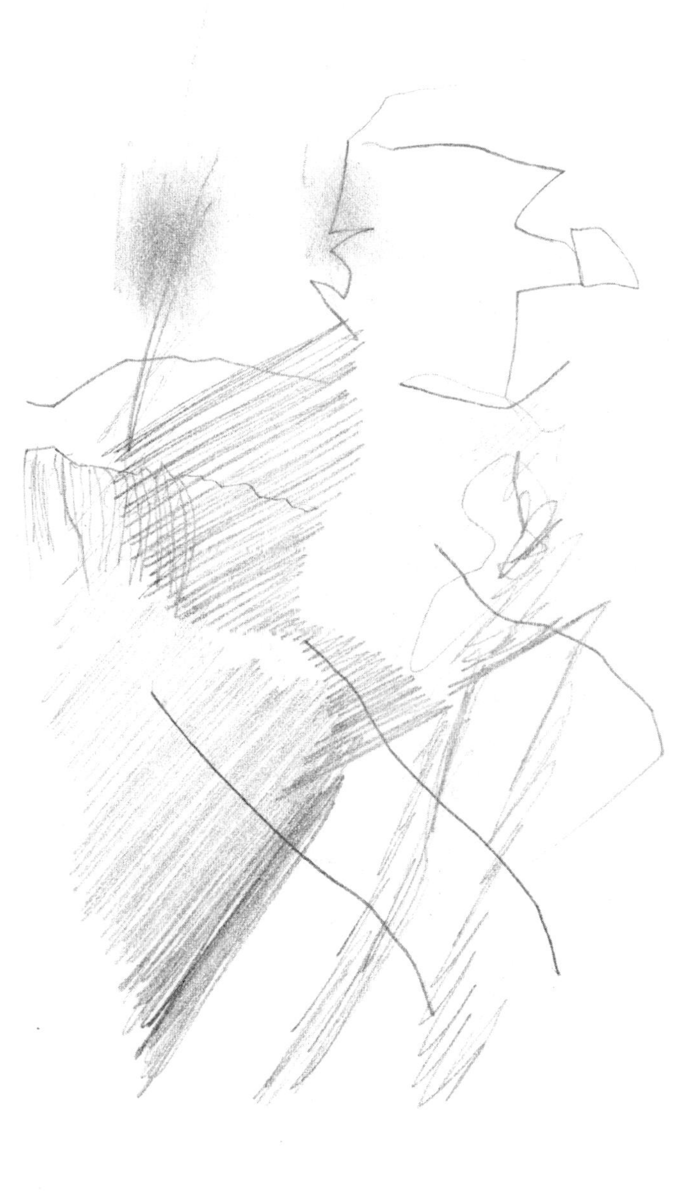

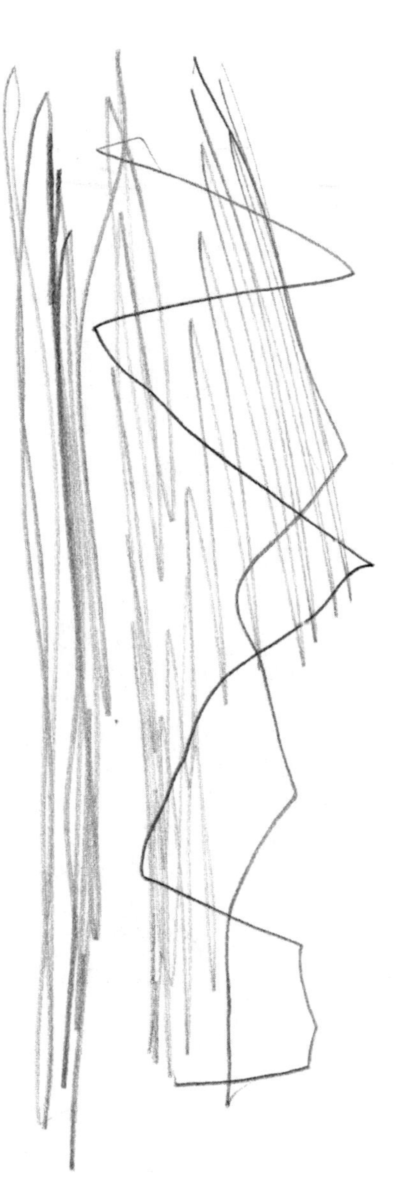

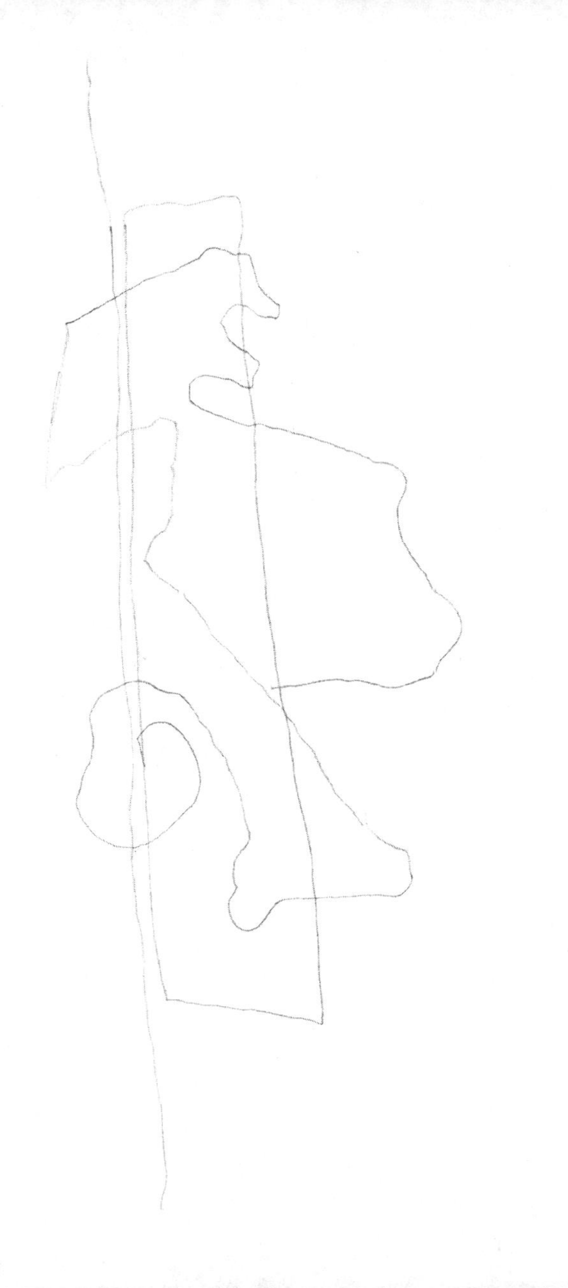

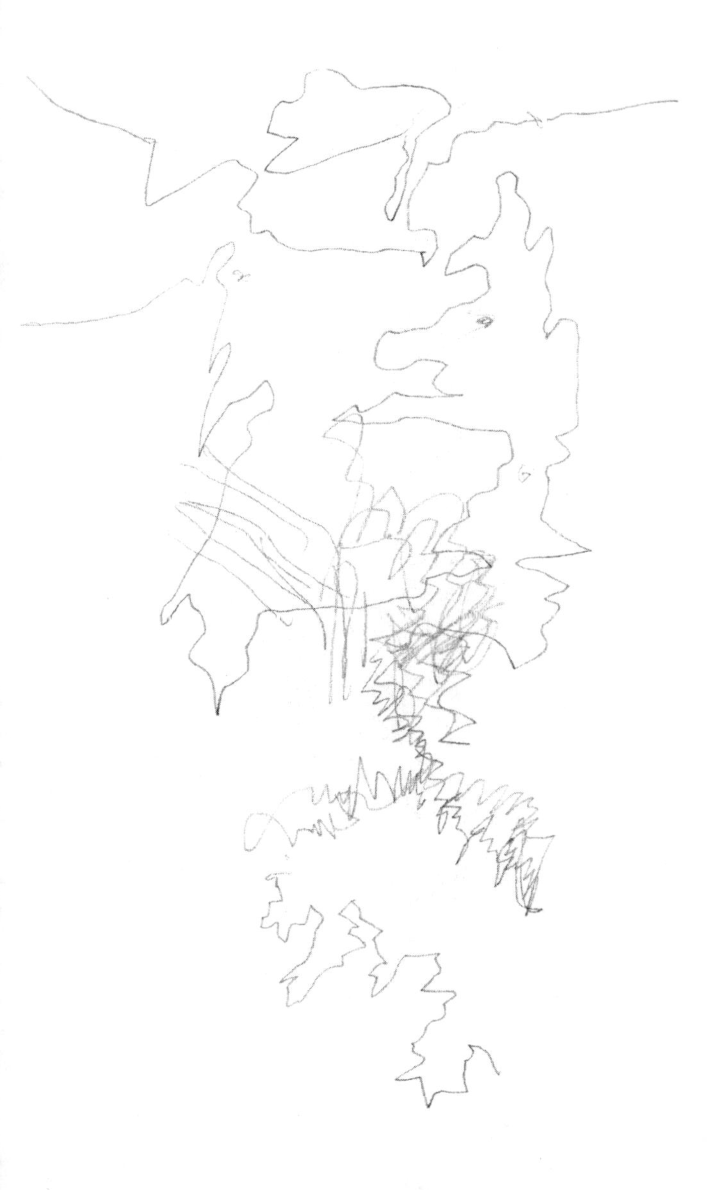

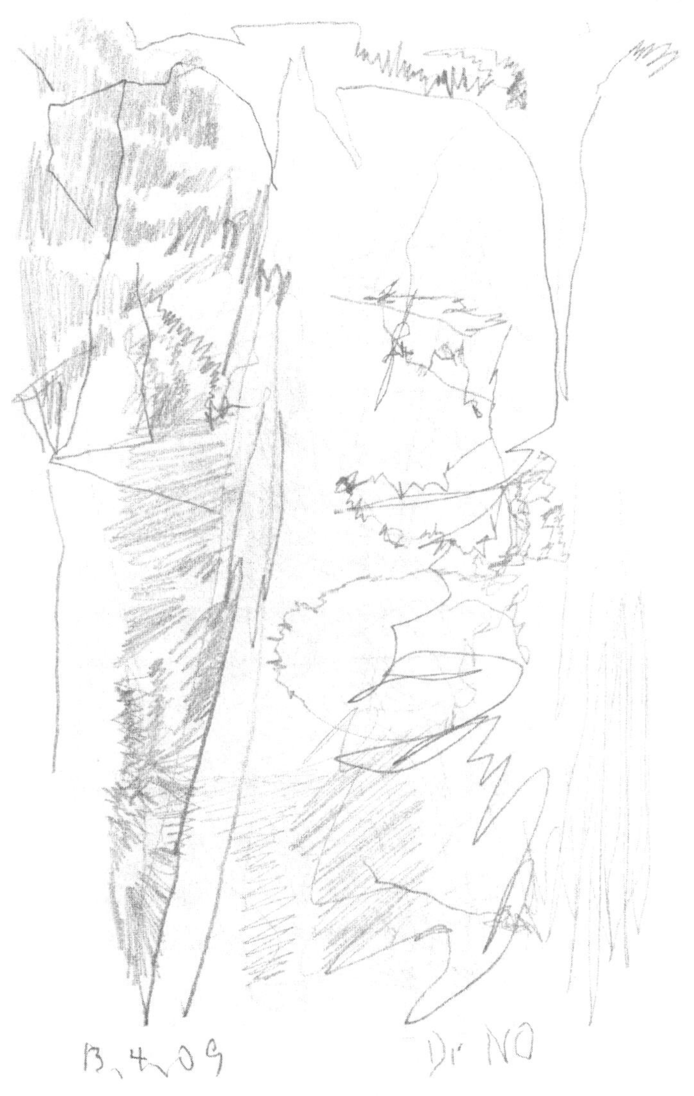
13.4.09
Dr NO

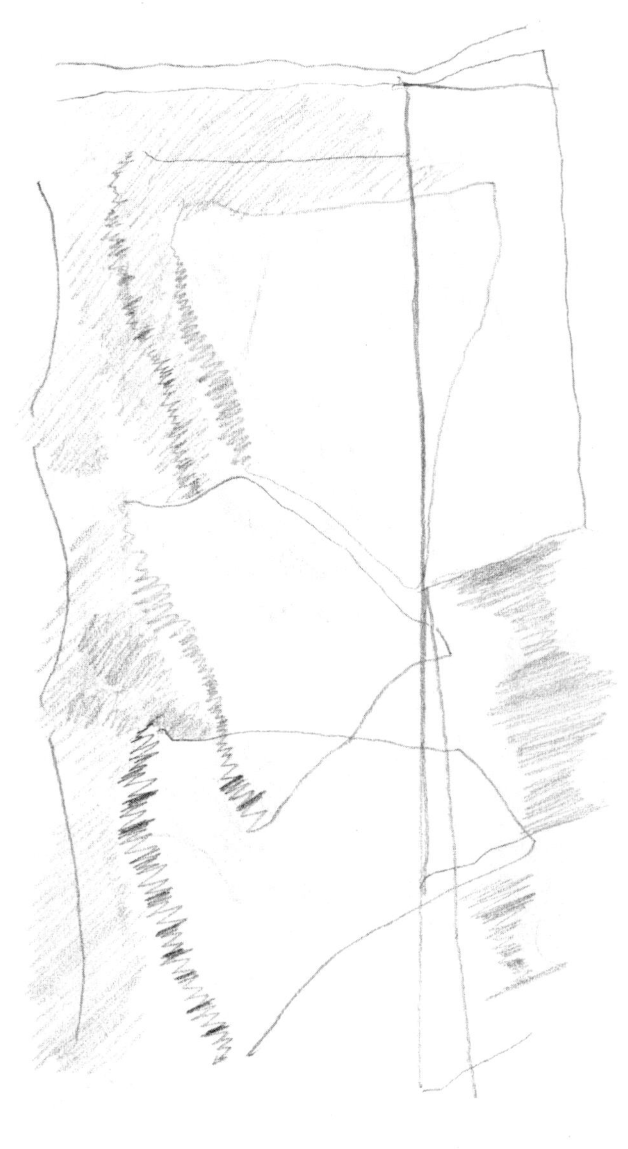

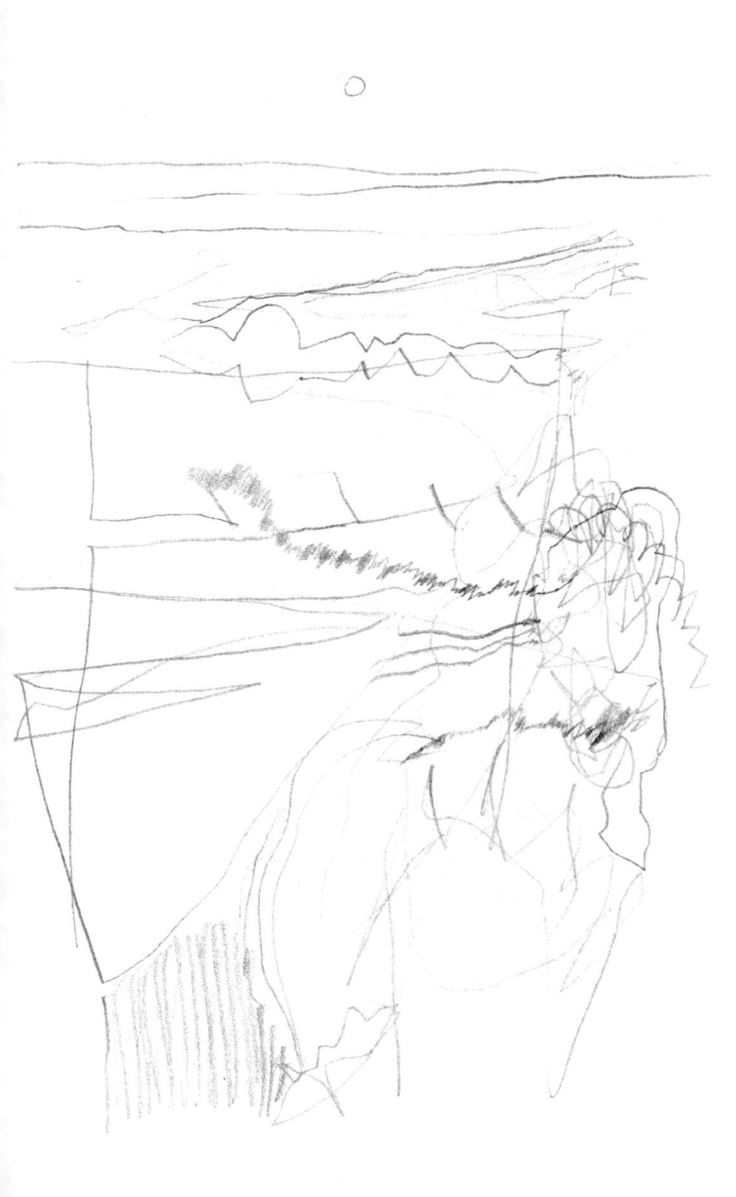

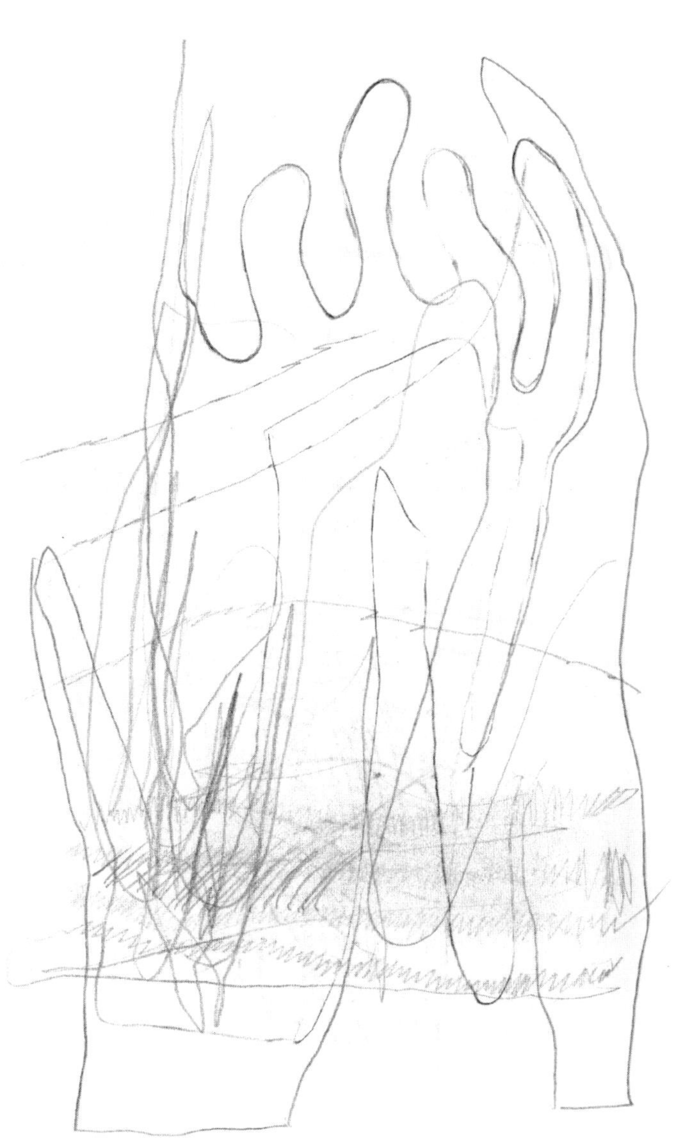

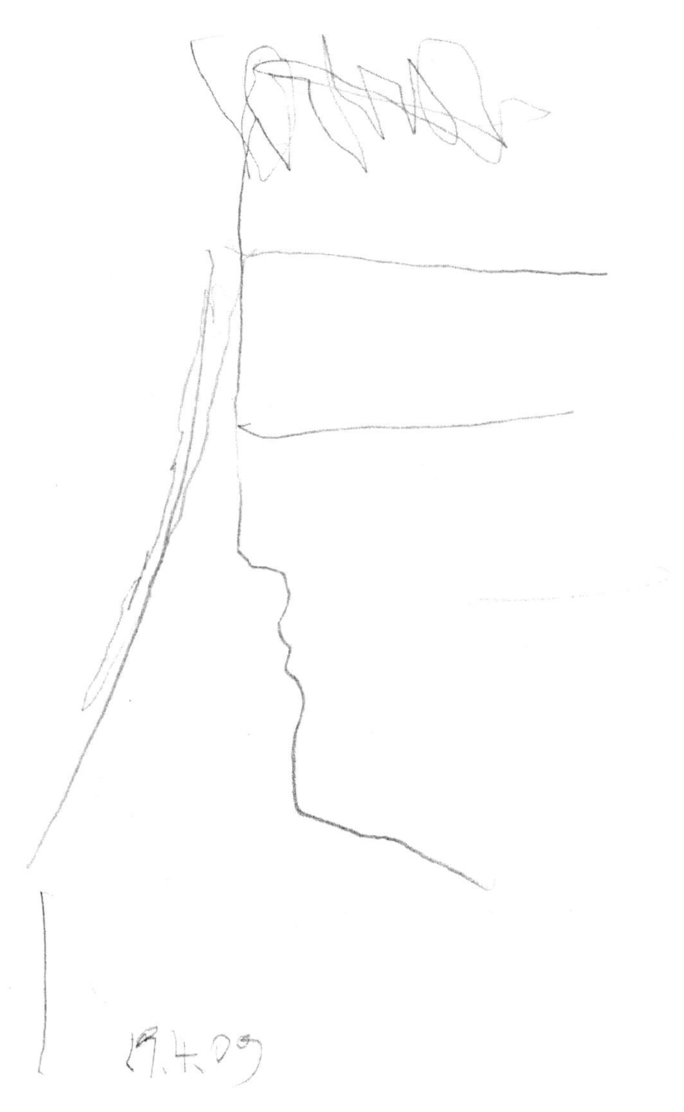
19.4.09

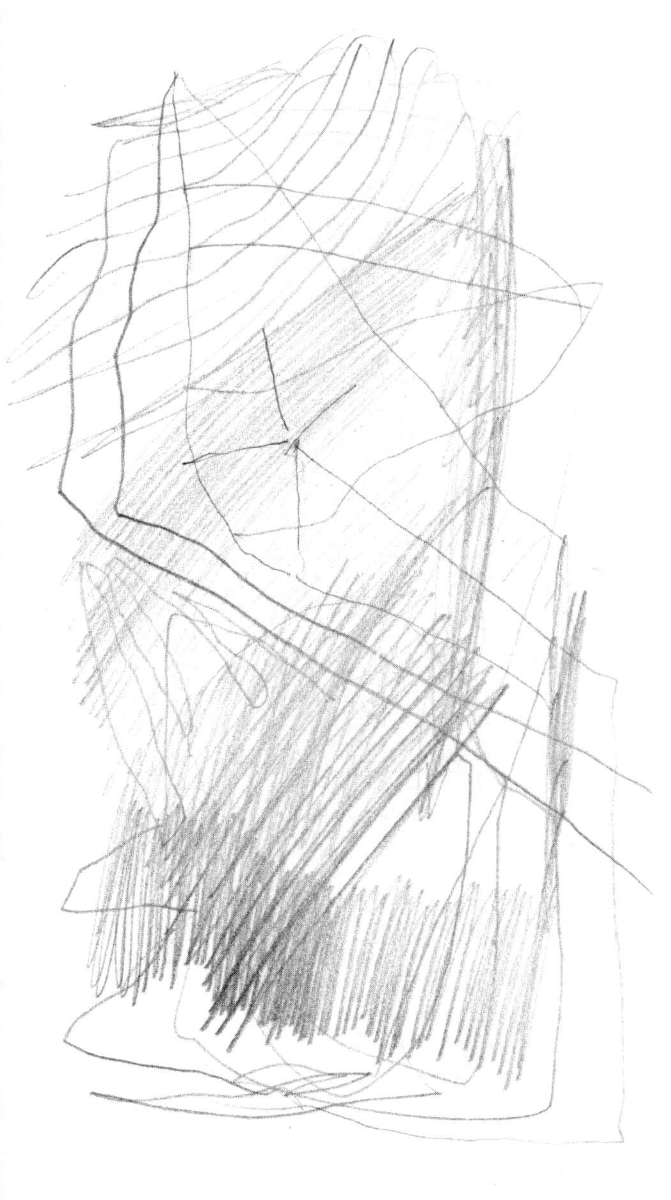

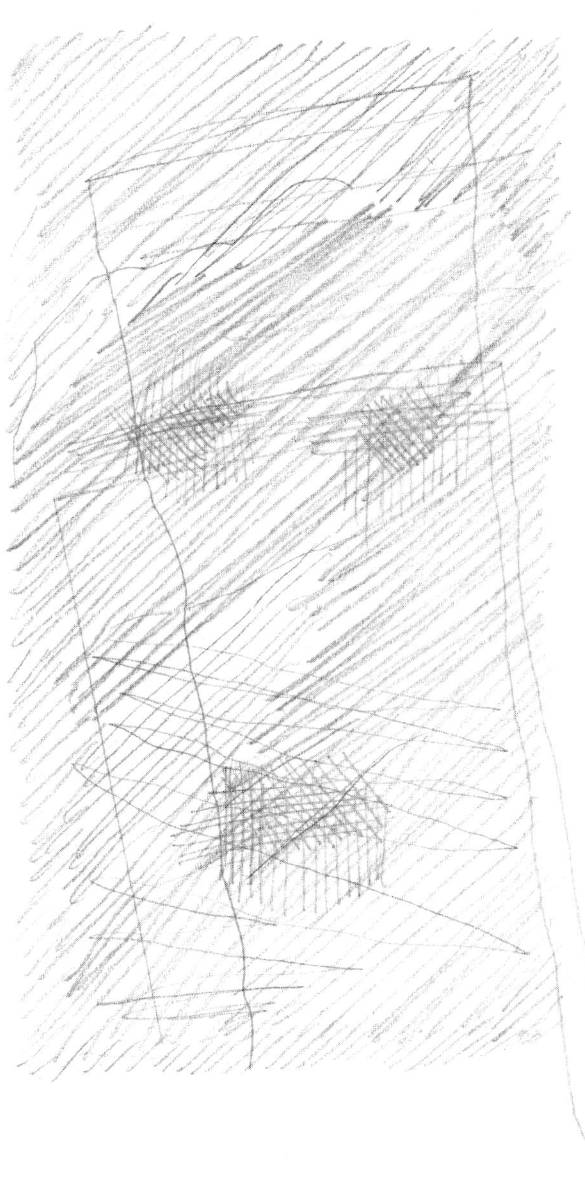